AF226882

God Instances

Books by Ruby F. Nazaruk

Story Collections

Words In All Their Splendor
A String Called Love
A Journey of People & Ourselves
Do You Have a Pen?
A Trail of What if's & Love
The Author's Mind
Bedtime Stories for Children
Leaves & Their Whispers

Ruby's Faith Collection

A Journey with Our Lady

Ruby's Learning Collection

Living Life with Dyslexia

God
Instances

Faith Moves Mountains.

RUBY F. NAZARUK

Copyright © 2024 Ruby Nazaruk

Copyright © All Photos & Images

All rights reserved.

ISBN: 978-1-7381794-2-8

DEDICATION

In Loving Memory of Rudy Dupilka and
Betty Hermanson, two people who taught me
a great deal about Faith.

CONTENTS

AUTHORS NOTE

This book is for all those looking for God. For those trying to find the sign or answer they are looking for. I am no expert, yet I know God can use us as His instruments.

So, I hope that with this book, God might use me to answer a prayer or touch one's life to bring them closer to God.

If you are waiting for a sign, do not give up. Keep trusting God. He will give you an answer; it just might not be the way you expect.

Our faith journeys are different, and our cross-to-bear will differ from others. God has a reason and purpose for all the things we go through.

I have been blessed with the toolbox of faith, but I am not perfect. We are all sinners, and we all make mistakes. The Saints have been my truest companions and trusted friends, and I look forward to introducing them to you. Without my faith, I would not have made it this far.

ACKNOWLEDGMENTS

This book would not have been possible without those who supported me in my spiritual and faith journeys.
Thank you for helping me learn more about my faith, being Catholic, and what it means to trust God.
For my parents, who have strived to give me a faith-filled toolbox.

1 GOD MOMENTS

"For I know the Plans that I have for you, Declares the Lord." (Jeremiah 29:11).

God Instances is a collection of real stories from my life showcasing how God can work in our lives. I set out to capture all the moments God has blessed me with.

Through these stories, I hope that God will speak to you or that something within this collection will speak to your heart.

For those unfamiliar with the term God Instances or God Moments. God Instances or Moments can come when we least expect them or need them the most.

These are the times we feel closer to God, and we can see with our own eyes in the physical world how he is working within our lives.

Moments are small and yet have the biggest impact. While God Moments or Instances can be few and far between, they are always such a gift.

I have been very blessed to experience God Moments throughout my life, so I desire to share these moments with others.

These can come in all shapes and forms. They could be a person, an answered prayer, or a friend's gift.

Think of the moments when something happens that makes everything better or moments that cannot quite be explained—all these Instances where God is working and touching our lives.

Sometimes, we get so busy in life that we miss them when we are not paying attention, or perhaps we are not looking for them.

Take time to look for these moments. You might be surprised by what you see or how God works within your life.

I have never been one to plan too far into the future, for God's plans are always far better than mine.

Let God direct your life.

Waiting on the Lord for an answer can be hard, and yet, there is not much one cannot learn by waiting.

May God bless you, and may your life be filled with many God instances! Amen.

BASILICA OF THE VISITATION ANNECY, FRANCE, 2008.

It all begins with Him, His Church, His Life, and His Death. God's Moments or Instances start and end with Him, and He is the center of all of it. He is writing our stories.

2 THE BEGINNING.

"But Jesus said, "Let the little children come to Me, and do not forbid them; for of such is the kingdom of heaven." (Matthew 19:14).

All stories have a beginning. Our Catholic journey begins at our Baptism.

Our stories start as infants and our journey in life, just as Christ's journey on earth started with his birth and ours.

The gift of Baptism begins the journey in the Catholic faith for most Catholics, at least those of us who are cradle-to-grave Catholics. From the time we are born, God works within us. He is with us at the beginning and the end.

While I do not remember my own Baptism as I was just a baby. I like to think of how my journey with God began then. We are all children of God, and he works within us.

The beginning of life is that of a child's cries—the gift of life and children from God.

While everyone's journey is different, we all begin as babies and start the life of being

Catholic through our Baptism.

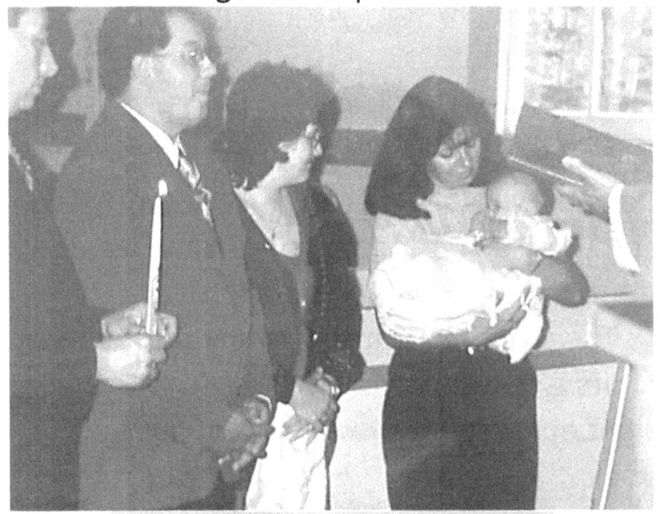

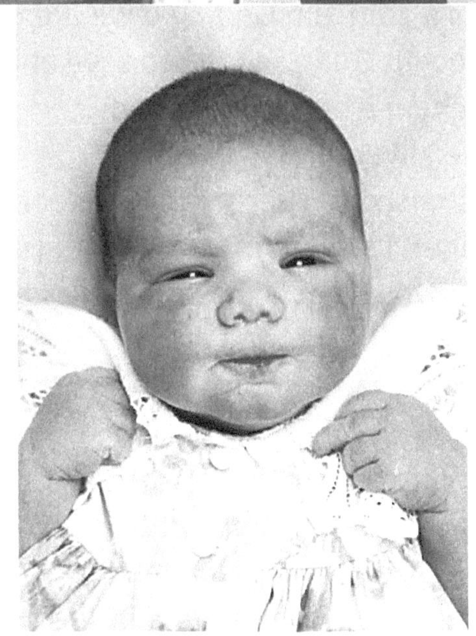

REMEMBER, YOU ARE A CHILD OF GOD!

3 THE BEAUTY OF LIFE

Life is a beautiful gift, and it is precious. We do not always know how much time we have or will get. Life can be very short, and sometimes, it ends too soon. However, it all goes according to God's plan.

The one thing worth fighting for the most in life is the unborn. The most vulnerable right now are those who do not have a voice.

Life is a gift from God, and we are called to protect it. God used me to save children and to change hearts and minds.

I have always been pro-life.

I was raised to cherish and respect life. As a teenager, I started my pro-life journey by getting involved in activism, such as the March for Life and Life Chains.

When my family moved to Edson, I got involved with the prolife group and had the opportunity to be a voice for the voiceless.

I was still unsure of my life's direction when I graduated high school.

I have since learned that our life's direction is ever-changing; like a ship upon the ocean, you never know how the ocean's waters will change.

I applied for mission jobs and ministry, yet none of that worked out.

It was not where I was meant to be, so when the Canadian Center for Bioethical Reform- CCBR internship arose, it was one of those moments of Why not?

I was unsure what I was getting myself into, yet I knew it would be important. When everything fell into place, I knew God was saying yes to this path.

It led to two internships with CCBR, one primarily in Calgary and another a traveling internship that took me to Vancouver, Manitoba, and other places.

After my first internship, I got a job as executive director for the Edson Friends for Life pro-life group where I lived.

The path was clear, and this work needed to be done.

Those days during my internship were some of the hardest and most challenging days I have ever faced.

Yet the internships taught me so much, not just about standing up against abortion; I learned more about myself as a person. I learned how to find common ground and have difficult discussions.

The topic is not a comfortable topic; then again, abortion should never be a comfortable topic to discuss because we are talking about the death of innocent unborn children.

When it comes to activism, one will meet all sorts of people with vast backgrounds and beliefs.

EDSON, LIFE CHAIN, OCTOBER 2011.

<u>Prayer To Protect Life</u>

Dear Lord
Look kindly on all the unborn whom You
have called to life.
From the moment of their conception,
protect all innocent unborn children whose
hearts begin to beat at an early stage of
pregnancy. They are those who can serve
You for a lifetime on earth and praise and
love You for all eternity. Give their mothers
the means to bring these babies into the
world. Provide them with the insight to
know that even though they may not be
able to feed, clothe, and educate them,
someone is willing to adopt them and give
them the love they need.
Give both the mothers and their unborn
babies health of mind and body.
Help all their family members to be
accepting of this gift of new life, so that
they will be able to encourage the mother
and father and support them in any
necessary way.
Amen.

4 PRO-LIFE

Abortion, to some people, is a means to an end; to others, it is simply just a word. To us in the pro-life life movement abortion is, abortion is the killing of an innocent human being; abortion is a human rights violation people need to be educated on.

I remember the day I first learned about abortion; at the time, I did not realize how it would impact my life. I had no idea of abortion's existence because I was just a kid.

My family went to an event that happened to have a pro-life table.

My mom and I were checking out the table, and I became distracted by the baby display, which showed babies at different ages in the womb.

I recall my mom starting to cry and went to see why. I did not know she was looking at AVP (Abortion Victim Photography).

However, I could comprehend that I was looking at a dead baby and could not understand why.

In my innocent mind, my only conclusion was that I was looking at a miscarried baby as I knew of miscarriages, since my mom had previously had them.

I was confused as to why someone would want to bring up that kind of painful memory. I asked my mom about the images, and she then explained to me what abortion was and the reason the images were there.

To me, abortion is not just a word; it is a reminder that every day, three hundred lives are snatched from this world within this country. That is 100,000 abortions per year in Canada.

Abortion is not an easy topic to talk about or comfortable to speak about, nor should it be.

The truth about abortion is that it is a horrific injustice happening within our country. How can one not act?

How can we stand by as innocent lives are being lost?

Learning about abortion made me realize just how much life is a gift.

I am so thankful I have had the opportunity to speak out and help others learn how to be an advocate for the preborn.

When I first became active in the prolife movement, I was told it was not possible to make a difference and that I, as one person, could not change anything; those people were wrong. It is possible to make a difference and save lives.

I have been blessed to experience and observe others I interned with as they compassionately conversed with people walking by.

That moment when hearts and minds transform, whether it be a complete 180, a halfway change, or even just a slight change, all brings them one step closer: it all matters.

Our work and time are never wasted, even if all we save is just one life, because life is precious, and change is possible.

We must be willing to be a voice for the voiceless.

While many moments have stuck with me from my internships, a particular day during my first internship helped me continue on the hardest days.

While doing Activism, a woman who had

been staring at my sign for a while approached me and asked for a pamphlet.

She thanked me for my actions and asked if we were the same people with the big truck.

She went on to explain that the previous day, she was driving with her friend, who was pregnant and planning on having an abortion, and our truck pulled up beside them in traffic.

She explained that upon seeing the truck, her friend changed her mind and decided to go through with the pregnancy.

Just as she finished sharing this story with me, the truck drove by again, and she said that because of our truck, her friend would be having her baby.

The moments we experience where God uses us as His instruments can be the most beautiful.

There are times when we do not realize the effects of our actions or the small moments that impact others.

However, there are these God-instances where we witness or hear of the impact or changes, we made on someone else's life.

CCBR INTERNSHIP, 2017,
CHOICE CHAIN

If you want to know more or are interested in getting involved, please visit: **https://www.endthekilling.ca/.**

If you are looking for reading material. *Seeing is Believing* by Jonathon Van. Maren, *The Culture War* by Jonathon Van. Maren, or *Stuck* by Justina Van Manen.

Prayer to St. Gianna for the Protection of Unborn Children

Most Holy Saint Gianna, loving mother, and faithful servant of God, we humbly pray for your intercession in protecting the lives of unborn children.
Through your selfless and suffering motherhood, you have shown us the sanctity and beauty of human life.
We ask, dear Holy Servant, that you guide and inspire all mothers committed to respecting and cherishing the precious gift of new life.
Heavenly Father, we implore your grace and wisdom upon those who face difficult decisions regarding pregnancy so that they may choose life and embrace the joy of motherhood.
Through your powerful intercession, Saint Gianna, may all unborn children be safeguarded and families be strengthened in love.
In Jesus Christ's name, we pray.
Amen.

5 ST. GIANNA

"The secret of happiness is to live moment by moment and to thank God for all that He, in His goodness, sends to us day after day." St. Gianna.

While I have many friendships with different saints, Saint Gianna has held a special place in my heart since my Confirmation.

St. Gianna Beretta Molla is my confirmation saint and a great inspiration in my pro-life work over the years.

Saint Gianna was a doctor, a profoundly devoted catholic, and a mother.

St. Gianna and her husband wrote love letters their whole lives; they had a beautiful marriage and family, and their love for Christ was immense.

After their deaths, their daughter published the collection of letters between Gianna and her husband, Pietro.

I was overjoyed when I received a copy of the book from my mom, which Gianna's daughter signed.

St. Gianna has taught me so much about love through her letters to her husband and the love and sacrifice she made for her children.

She taught me love, sacrifice, and trust in God and his plan. She was a doctor who strove to protect life.

She emulated empathy and compassion.

In her last pregnancy, she developed a fibroma on her uterus.

She had to make a choice: her life or the life of her unborn child. She chose her daughter's life.

After her daughter was born, she attempted to treat the fibroma; however, she developed septic peritonitis only a week after giving birth and died.

Her husband wrote her biography, and they named their daughter Gianna Emanuela after her mother.

Gianna, being a doctor and a mother, understood the value of life and the choices she was making.

When I was doing a traveling internship with CCBR for pro-life activism, we ended up being in Manitoba for a while.

While there, I had the opportunity to visit

the church dedicated to her.

They also had a beautiful statue of her and a relic.

It was amazing to connect on a deeper level with her as I connected to the saints I saw while in France when I was young. Building relationships with the Saints is a beautiful thing. **WINNIPEG, MANITOBA 2018.**

St. Gianna's Prayer

Jesus, I promise You to submit myself to
all that You permit to befall me,
Make me only know Your will.
My most sweet Jesus,
infinitely merciful God, most tender
Father of souls,
and in a particular way of the most weak,
most miserable,
most infirm
which You carry with special tenderness
between Your divine arms,
I come to You to ask You,
through the love and merits of Your
Sacred Heart,
the grace to comprehend and to always do
Your holy will,
the grace to confide in You,
The grace to rest securely through time and
eternity in Your loving, divine arms.
Amen.

<u>Prayer to St. Gianna for the Strengthening of Marriages</u>

*Dearest St. Gianna called to be a witness
of God's love through your generous
sacrifice,
I humbly ask for your intercession.
Strengthen the bond of my marriage and
help us to embody the love of Christ.
May we always cherish the gift of our
union and follow your example of
selflessness in serving our family and
suffering fellow men.
Through your heavenly aid,
may we be steadfast in our love, grow in
faith, and obtain graces to overcome life's
challenges.
In Jesus' name,
Amen.*

Novena To Obtain Graces Through Saint Gianna Beretta Molla

God, our Father, You have granted to Your church the gift of Gianna Beretta Molla. In her youth, she lovingly sought You and drew other young people to You, involving them, through apostolic witness and Catholic Action, in the care of the sick and aged to help and comfort them.

We thank You for the gift of this young woman, so deeply committed to You. Through her example, grant us the grace to consecrate our lives to Your service for the joy of our brothers and sisters.

Glory be ...

Jesus, Redeemer of mankind, You called Saint Gianna to exercise the medical profession as a mission for the comfort of bodies and souls. In her suffering fellow men and in the little ones, deprived of all support, she saw You. We thank You for having revealed Yourself to this servant as "one who serves" and who soothes the sufferings of men. Treasuring her example may we become generous Christians at the service of our brothers and sisters, especially those with whom You deign to share Your Cross.

Glory be...

God, Sanctifying Spirit, who loves the Church as Your Bride, You poured into the heart of Saint Gianna a share of Your Love so that she could radiate it in her family and thus cooperate with You in the wonderful plan of creation, and give life to new children who could know and love You.

We thank You for this model wife and, through her encouraging witness, we beg You to grant to our families the serene and Christian presence of mothers committed to transform their homes into cenacles of faith and love, rich with generous activity and sanctifying service.

Glory be...

O God, Creator and lover of mankind, You were close to Saint Gianna when, affected by illness, she was in the painful dilemma of choosing between her own life and the life of the child whom she was carrying in herself, a gift long-awaited.

Trusting You alone, and aware of Your Commandment to respect human life, Gianna found the courage to do her duty as a mother and to say "yes" to the new life of her baby, generously sacrificing her own.
Through the intercession of Mary, Mother of Jesus, and after the example of Gianna, all mothers are inspired to welcome with love the sparkle of new life. Grant us the grace we are praying for .... and the joy of finding Inspiration in Saint Gianna, who, as a model spouse and mother, after the example of Christ, gave up her life for the life of others.

Hail Mary...

Amen.

SAINT GIANNA, PRAY AND INTERCEDE FOR US!

6 GOD MOVES IN US

God moves in us in many ways. The world can be challenging, and it can be hard to know what direction to take. Sometimes, we will not know until we feel God move in us.

Until we feel that prompting that urges us forward when we least expect it.

When we feel the Holy Spirit come into our lives and guide us in our direction, let God move us where we need to go.

When you do not know what direction to go, pray and wait. Let God guide you. Open your hearts and minds to him, come to Jesus, pray, and ask that he will come into your life.

When God is moving and working in us, we do not always see it firsthand.

We will not always know how small moments in our lives have greatly impacted others. However, the moments we get to see glimpses of God working within or through us, using us as his instruments, can be such an amazing gift.

2015.

Let God move within you. Be open to him and his will. Listen to what he whispers to your heart. Jesus, I open my heart and whole self to you. Move within me, Amen.

7 EMBRACING MOMENTS

Embracing the quiet moments and silent times one has been given, whether it is while one is knitting or doing some small work or just sitting and basking in the silence and spending the time to draw oneself closer to the Lord in those moments.

The small moments matter the most to me because when combined, they become one massive thing bigger than a single big moment. I will always try to be thankful for the trivial things and moments I am granted.

Often, it is the small things that matter most. As St. Thérèse has taught me, the little way, and throughout my life, the little moments, the glimpses of Christ within my life. Learning to embrace these small moments is a beautiful thing. I encourage you to follow the trail of breadcrumbs of little moments laid out inside your lives.

Some moments will change the trajectory of our lives—unexpected moments. These are the moments we can draw closer to

Christ and feel his love, which makes our hearts leap for joy.

While I can think of many moments in which I have felt Christ in my life, God Instances and Moments that have shaped me into the person I am today. One that stands out is December 19th, 2004, the day of my First Communion. I remember how my heart leaped for joy that day and moment.

Fr. Lucien Morrissette is another person who inspired my faith greatly as a child. He was my parish priest for a long time and will always be fondly remembered.

What is the moment that made your heart leap for joy?

At St. Gabriel's, students would craft a cross for First Communion classes. My Grandfather helped me craft mine.

I still have it, and when I see it, I think of the journey for my First Communion and of the early seeds of faith planted.

The flickering light of an ember has now become a burning flame, a light for Christ.

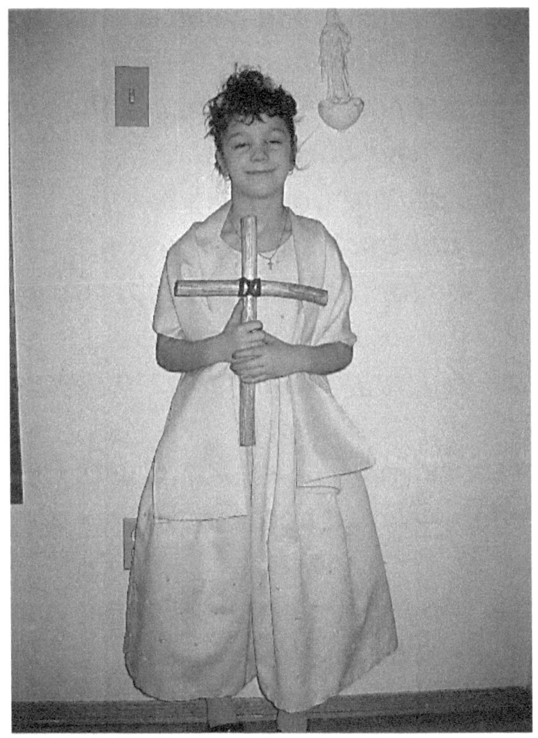

MY FIRST COMMUNION CROSS AND DRESS 2004.

A Prayer of Thanksgiving

Loving and compassionate God,
God of infinite goodness and mercy,
Your blessed name be glorified.
Yours is the glory,
You are the ruler of all the land and
everything on it;
You are the ruler of the world and all its
inhabitants.
God, of all of us, teach us to live the way
we have always wanted.
You are our God and Savior,
And our trust is always in you.
We thank you for the blessings that you give
us every day.
We thank you for providing food to those in
need.
We thank you for blessing us with the
desire for your justice for those who are
poor.
We thank you for blessing us with the voice
to speak for the voiceless.
We thank you for allowing us to be your
hands and feet in the world,
For the blessing of being part of the great
family that is your Church.

Hear our prayer and help us always remember your call to justice and compassion.
Our God, you will conquer all injustice; with your help, we will be victorious.
Amen.

An Act of Love
O my God because you are infinite goodness and worthy of infinite love, I love you with my whole heart above all things, and for love of you, I love my neighbor as myself.
Amen.

An Act of Hope
O my God, trusting in your promises and because you are faithful, powerful, and merciful, I hope, through the merits of Jesus Christ, for the pardon of my sins, final perseverance, and the blessed glory of heaven. Amen.

<u>*(John 6:53-58).*</u>

Jesus said to them,
"Very truly I tell you, unless you eat the
flesh of the Son of Man and drink his blood,
You have no life in you.
Whoever eats my flesh and drinks my
blood has eternal life, and I will raise them
up at the last day.
For my flesh is real food, and my blood is
real drink.
Whoever eats my flesh and drinks my
blood remains in me, and I in them.
Just as the living Father sent me and I
live because of the Father,
so, the one who feeds on me will live
because of me.
This is the bread that came down from
heaven.
Your ancestors ate manna and died, but
whoever feeds on this bread will live
forever."

An Act of Faith.

*Oh my God, I firmly believe that you are
one God in three Divine Persons. Father,
Son, and Holy Spirit;
I believe that your Divine Son became
Man and died for our sins.
That He will come to judge the living and
the dead.
I believe in these and all the truths which
the Holy Catholic Church teaches,
because you have revealed to them who
can neither deceive nor be deceived.
Amen.*

8 FAITH

"You have faith like a grain of mustard seed; you will say to this mountain, 'Move from here to there,' and it will move. Nothing will be impossible for you." (Matthew 17:20).

Faith comes in many shapes and forms. We cannot give our faith to others. Faith can be as small as the grain of mustard seed. Faith can move mountains. Faith is a beautiful foundation. It shapes us and draws us closer to Christ. Faith is like a compass guiding us through uncertainties and challenges in our lives.

Faith is not something others can give us but something we have to gain and discover on our own. We can be taught about our faith and given the tools we need to build it up, but in the end, it is up to us to want to choose that faith.

We are given the tools of life and told of the lord. It does not mean we always have faith. It means we have the possibility to believe. With hope, there is faith. With faith, there is love.

Faith that our prayers have been heard and answered.

We whisper prayers in the dark as we wait for sleep to come.

We light candles of prayer offerings, offering up the burning light for those in our prayers or the intentions within our hearts.

Faith can be hard sometimes. It involves believing in things you cannot see, yet if we really look, we can see the Lord all around us.

Be a Light of Faith wherever you go, like a flickering candle to the world.

CANDLES IN LOURDES, FRANCE 2008.

9 SIGNS

"How great are his signs! and how mighty are his wonders! his kingdom is an everlasting kingdom, and his dominion is from generation to generation." (Daniel 4:3).

There are times when we pray, ask God to give us a sign, and we wait. Sometimes, we receive a clear sign; other times, it is more subtle, and if we are not looking, we miss it; other times, we may wait, and it does not appear until it suddenly does. It can be when we least expect it. However, there are times we do not get a sign for whatever reason, mostly because God has something better in mind for us.

There once was a lady who prayed for a sign and asked the Lord to show one. She struggled to feel his love and felt like her prayers fell on deaf ears. She continued to pray and asked for a Sign that showed the love He had for her, for it seemed as though he was not there.

There are times we all have felt like God is ever so far away from us. We wonder if we are being heard and why we go through things. We can feel alone and wonder where God has gone and why he has left us.

One Saturday at church, she prayed again for God to give her a sign. The Lady received her answer in the most unexpected way: a little girl and a wax crayon drawing.

That Saturday after mass, a little girl came up to her. In her hands, she held a single sheet of paper. She said Excuse me, I made this drawing, and you are supposed to have it.

The Lady reached out and took the drawing from the little girl. It was a simple drawing and not overly remarkable, and yet the lady cried tears of joy, for she received her sign and, at that moment, felt God's love all around her. At the top of the page where the big yellow sun was, the little girl had written four words upon the page: Smile, God Loves You.

Her sign came in the form of a little girl and a wax crayon drawing, and in many ways, it changed how the lady saw God's love for her. It also showed the little girl how God can use even the smallest of people or things to make a difference, how four words on a page could make such a big impact.

The little girl once drew a crayon drawing, not the first or the last, but one of her many drawings as a child. Yet this one was different. It had a purpose, and it was intended for someone. She did not know who. It was a Friday night, and she was drawing before bed like she often did. She had just finished drawing this house, and a big bright yellow sun was in the top corner. When she felt that she needed to write four words and only four, she wrote the words and smiled to herself. The next morning, as she was getting ready for church, she knew she needed to bring the drawing with her. All through church, she wondered who it was for and whom she was supposed to give it to.

Then mass ended, and she saw the lady and knew that she was supposed to give it to her. She approached the lady and said Excuse me, I made this drawing, and you are supposed to have it. The lady thanked her and said she was sweet. The lady took the drawing and burst into tears. At a loss, the little girl turned to her mom; what had she done wrong?

Seeing her distress, the lady wiped her tears and said these are happy tears, for you brought me the sign for which I have been praying. I have prayed to know God loves me, and today, you showed me that he does.

God used a little girl and a wax crayon drawing to show his love and give a sign. Sometimes, it is the most unexpected way that he speaks to us. It can be an actual sign, a person, or a feeling. Whatever it is, when it is the right time, it will be revealed to us.

Time passed, and the lady grew older, as did the little girl. The girl would visit the lady occasionally, and after the drawing, the lady and the girl became friends.

The little girl would always pause and smile in the hall upon entering and leaving at the lady's home, for upon the wall in a plain brown frame hung a wax crayon drawing with a child's writing and a reminder that love is always around, even when it is unseen.

The girl has grown up now, and the lady has gone away to the Father in heaven, yet even as time passed, the girl thought of the lady fondly and remembered how four words changed everything.

The lady in this story prayed for a sign and received one. When I pray and wait for a sign, I try to wait patiently, yet it can be difficult. I think of the lady in this story when it is hard, and I do not seem to get an answer.

The story is real, and the lady's name was Betty Hermanson, and I was the little girl who drew a wax crayon drawing.

I remember when Betty got sick; she was hospitalized after a bad stroke, and I went with my mom to see her. I was going through a phase where I loved pocket things, crosses, pocket prayers, and pocket angels. I had this angel in a clear circle, like a rock.

I remember how hard Betty was struggling, and I remember reaching into my pocket, taking her hand, and placing it into hers. The smile she gave me was radiant. She kept it with her like she did the crayon drawing until she died a few years later. I do not know what happened to the Crayon drawing or the pocket angel after she passed away. I hope they ended up going to someone who needed it. I still think about it over the years and how simple it was, how powerful it was, and how God used me as his instrument.

Betty will always have a place in my heart, and I will always be grateful that I had the opportunity to be a part of something bigger than myself.

While I do not have many things from Betty, I learned about faith, waiting, and trust in God from her. I learned that signs are not always just signs and that they can be the most unexpected things. The one thing I have always cherished is the card she gave me a short while after I gave her the wax crayon drawing. Her words always say it best.

March 5, 2006

Dear Ruby,
Thank you so very much for the wonderful thoughts you wrote and gave me on Saturday at Mass. It was just what I needed and had asked God about earlier. Nothing else could have been a better gift.
You are a gift from God.
God Bless You. Love, Betty.

Remember, Smile, God Loves You!

10 LOOKING BACK

When I was younger, I often found myself writing about the future and wondering what it would be like to look back upon my life and how it would change as I grew, and life happened.

"I want to look back on my life and the days I lived, and that I used every moment to the best of my ability.

I want to say I danced like no one was watching, smiling, and laughing despite sadness or pain.

I loved and cared about people and that people could see God through me and my actions. I want to be an example to others."

While I am now much older, I still find myself writing the same sorts of things, and yet, looking back, I can see it.

While we can get lost in the past if we spend too much time looking back, there is also much to learn from it.

Like how when we are younger, sometimes we know what we want to be when we grow up or at least have some idea of what we would like the future to be.

I find myself asking myself, what would the younger me think of this?

Looking back, I see that even today, I still want to live my life to the fullest.

When I was younger, I talked about smiling through the pain.

Years later, with the chronic battle of chronic illness and pain, while it can be challenging, I have learned to always keep smiling.

I still want to be an example and for others to see Christ within me.

So, ask yourself what younger me would say if they were with me right now. You might just be surprised at what comes to mind.

11 AUGUST 2012

I want my life to really mean
something. I want to make a difference,
even if it's not a very big one.
I want to change people's lives.
I want to live my life so that when
people see me, they see Jesus; they see
him in me, and they see how much he is
worth having faith in.
How much he can change people. I
want to do God's will.
I know I am not perfect, and I know I
am going to make mistakes, but I also
know Jesus is always waiting to forgive
our sins, even if we think we have too
much to send for him to forgive.
Sometimes, I wonder what God has
planned for me and what he wants me to
do with my life.
Questions swirl in my head, and I do
not have the answers, nor can I find them.
What am I supposed to do with my life?
Who does he want me to be?
I am searching for myself.
I know I am meant to do great things
and have a purpose, but I feel lost at times
and unsure that I'm doing anything right.

Reflecting on the past while I have grown, I can still see so many questions, answers, and lessons to be sought.

While I am still searching for the purpose the Lord has for me in this older me, looking back at the younger me, I see just how far I have come.

Lord, speak through me. Help this book bring others closer to you so that they can recognize their own God instances within their own lives. Lord, I want to serve you so that I can use my gift of writing to help others. I continue to want my life to mean something, to make a difference.

May the Lord guide us all as we seek direction and to serve our life's purpose. We must all strive to learn more about our faith and live it out daily.

Thank you, Lord, for the opportunities you have blessed us with.

Please help us to continue to strive to share our faith with others and your gospel.

Amen.

12 IN HIS HANDS

"Behold, I have engraved thee upon the palms of my hands; thy walls are continually before me." (Isaiah 49.16. KJV).

Sometimes, God holds you back until the road is safe to continue. God holds us in the palms of his hand, guiding and leading us.

Sometimes, he challenges us to help strengthen us or to help us grow in some way.

There are times we plow ahead in life, get caught up in the whirlwind of life, and do not listen to or hear his guiding voice.

This is when he holds us back to put a halt on the direction we are heading.

It is like a parent stopping a child from rushing into a busy street at a crosswalk when it is unsafe to cross.

Or a lifeguard telling us not to run at the pool. It all has a reason and a purpose.

While we cannot always see the reasons God holds us back, there is a purpose to it.

I have learned that when things do not go my way, sometimes it is because they are not going in the direction I am supposed to be going. Remember that He holds you in His hands. He has a plan for you.

If we turn to him in need, He will wrap us up and protect us in His hands.

Life can be full of many amazing things, yet we can get distracted by a great deal of it.

So, when things are not going your way or in the direction you hoped, stop, and wonder what direction the Lord is trying to guide you.

Is the roadblock a moment for us to learn, or is God telling us to put on the brakes and re-evaluate our situation or directions?

13 CREATIONS

As my bare feet touched the cold, wet dirt, I felt like one of Jesus's apostles walking out on the sand. It felt magical and wonderful.

I looked up at the clouded blue sky lying in the green grass and thought my God, is awesome.

Jesus had made the world and his creations greater than all things.

I love the sound of the birds singing, the sound of my swing when I swing up and down, the sound of my little brothers playing and laughing, the sound of the Creek in the sounds of joy, and the sound of God's creations.

The smell of fresh flowers and the wind blowing in my hair, the sounds of geese and our dog running, the bees buzzing in the sounds of spring and summer.

The puddles splashed when I jumped in them or rode my bike through them. It is also wonderful: the smell and sounds of the rain are wonderful, the colors are shining, and the sky is crystal blue.

The sounds of waves on the beach, the light wind blowing my hair—they are all over the place. I love the earth; I love the way God made it and made us each so special.

The beauty of God's creations is all around us: in the stars that light up the night sky, in the wind, and in all the colors of the rainbow.

We are God's creations, and each of us is beautifully and uniquely made.

I sometimes wonder what it was like for the apostles and how they felt seeing the miracles God did, how they could fathom it all, and how it fits into the world and his existing creations.

I wonder if, in many ways, the apostles saw the world and its creations in a whole new light. Did their perspective on the meaning of different things change after their eyes were opened?

14 THE HABIT OF PRAYER

Developing a prayer habit can be challenging at first. Life can be very hectic and busy, and making time for prayer can be challenging when the world pulls us in every other direction.

Sadly, we cannot all live in a monastery or convent and have prayer be one of our sole focuses.

Yet taking the time to pray and sticking to it is vital for our spiritual life and spiritual health.

Start small. Choose a couple of prayers to say once daily, either morning or night and stick with them.

Once the habit forms, you can slowly add more prayers and devotions.

You can also start with a daily devotional that you can do for a full year.

A Prayer habit does not need to be complicated.

It simply needs to be regular and a time for you to draw closer to Christ.

15 A PRAYER ROUTINE

Over the years, we can grow and add things to our daily prayer routine, like a prayer suggested by a friend or a nighttime blessing that another family does.

Prayer can come in different forms and many other words.

A prayer routine ties to our habit of prayer.

Just like we have our daily routines for other things, we need to have a set prayer routine that is worked into our overarching daily routine.

Taking time to pray and communicate with God balances our day.

I begin and end my day with prayer. At the beginning of each year, I decide which prayers I will do for the morning and night of that year and stick with them.

Then, the following year, I can change it up. During the different seasons, such as Lent and Advent, one can add an adjusted routine to be even more connected during the special seasons within the church.

16 SPIRITUAL COMMUNION

Spiritual communion, a practice that unites oneself to Christ, is accessible to all. When the desire for union with Christ within the Eucharist arises, and one is unable to receive the Eucharist or attend mass physically, one can offer a spiritual communion.

This act prepares our hearts and minds to be united with Christ in spirit, regardless of our physical circumstances.

When we ask Christ to come to us, we open ourselves to his presence, becoming His tabernacles.

Spiritual communion is a personal act that enables us to receive a spiritual communion with Christ, opening a door for him to enter our hearts.

This personal connection with Christ guides us and strengthens our spiritual journey.

St. Alphonsus Liguori has a beautiful prayer for spiritual communion. If we cannot attend daily mass, we can pray for spiritual communion.

Spiritual Communion

Act of Spiritual Communion

My Jesus, I believe that you are present in the most blessed sacrament. I love you above all things, and I desire to receive you into my soul. Since I cannot at this moment receive you sacramentally, come at least spiritually into my heart. I embrace you as if you were already there when you unite myself wholly to you. Never permit me to be separated from you. Amen.

Another option when it comes to spiritual communion is realizing that our guardian angels are with us all the time.

If we are not attending mass, they are not attending mass because they are with us.

So, when you do your spiritual communion, also take time to send your Angel to mass on your behalf. You know our guardian angels are here to help us and guide us into life.

Many saints sent their guardian angels on various errands, such as praying in church and doing other things, and we can send our angels to pray and watch over other people for a brief time.

This specific prayer is for when you are unable to attend Holy Mass to send your Angel to church.

THE PRAYER
SEND YOUR ANGEL TO MASS

O holy angel, at my side,
Go to church for me,
Kneel in my place at Holy Mass
Where I desire to be.
At Offertory, in my stead,
Take all I am and own,
And place it as a sacrifice
Upon the Alter Throne.
At Holy Consecrations bell,
Adore with Seraph's love.
My Jesus hidden in the Host,
Come down from Heaven above.
And when the Priest, communion takes,
Oh, bring my Lord to me,
That His sweet heart may rest on mine,
And I His temple be.
Amen.

17 GUARDIAN ANGEL

The Catholic Catechism teaches us of Our Guardian Angels.

From infancy to death, human life is surrounded by their (guardian angels) watchful care and intercession. More about Angels can be found in the Catholic Catechism (CCC 336).

Beside each believer stands an angel as protector and shepherd, leading him or her to life in Heaven.

Already here on earth, the Christian life is shared by faith in the blessed company of angels and men united to God.

Our Guardian angels are always with us to guide and help protect us. As I said when talking about Spiritual Communion, we can send our angels to church when we cannot attend. We can also send our angels to someone in need of comfort or aid. Our angels are like invisible friends. God gives angels some of the most important roles.

So, when you are struggling, remember you can always ask your guardian angel for assistance. Some people even give their angels a name, and others, in times of great need, have even seen their angels.

GUARDIAN ANGEL, PRAY FOR US!

Guardian angel Prayer

Angel of God, my guardian dear, to whom God's love commits me here, ever this day [or night] be at my side, to light and guard, to rule and guide. Amen.

18 THE ARCH ANGELS

The Bible mentions archangels. God entrusts archangels with special duties, and they are recognized as leaders.

The Catechism states, "The existence of the spiritual, non-corporeal beings that Sacred Scripture usually calls 'angels' is a truth of faith," (Catechism of the Catholic Church, paragraph 328).

While the Bible in the church recognizes there are seven archangels. There are only three we know by name.

The three Arch Angels we know by name are:

The Messenger St. Gabriel. Gabriel means God is my strength.

The Protector St. Michael The Archangel. The name Michael means one who is like God.

The Guide St. Raphael. The name Raphael means God is my health.

The Feast of the Three Archangels is September 29th.

<u>ST. GABRIEL</u>

St. Gabriel is a messenger Angel to whom God entrusts important messages and missions.

Gabriel has appeared with messages to many within the bible.

He appeared to Daniel in the Old Testament.

He appeared to Zacharias, the father of John the Baptist.

To Elizabeth when she first conceived and again when she was six months pregnant.

He appeared to the Virgin Mary to bring the news. Gabriel said to Mary, "Hail, thou that art highly favored, the Lord is with thee: blessed art thou among women." Luke 1:28.

He is often represented with a trumpet, lilies, a sector, a shining lantern, and the colors blue and white.

St. Gabriel is the patron saint for messengers and postal workers.

ST. GABRIELL, MESSENGER OF GOD, PRAY FOR US!

Prayer to St. Gabriel for Intercession

*O Blessed Archangel Gabriel, we beseech thee, do thou intercede for us at the throne of divine Mercy
in our present necessities, that as thou didst announce to Mary the mystery of the Incarnation,
so, through thy prayers and patronage in heaven we may obtain the benefits of the same,
and sing the praise of God forever in the land of the living. Amen.*

As a Messager of God, we entrust our prayers and intersessions to your hands. Relay our request at the feet of Christ, our Lord.

Amen.

St. Michael the Archangel

St. Michael is our protector, soldier, and warrior. He helps in times of need when we feel unsafe, threatened, or endangered.

He can aid us when we feel temptations or the devil trying to pull us away from Christ.

St. Michael is an immensely powerful angel and protector. He battles against darkness, evil, temptations, and so much more.

I have grown up asking his intersession for protection, and whenever I am ever afraid, I turn to him. He can also aid us when we are angry or feeling overwhelmed.

He taught me that no battle is too great for our God and that God will protect us. That St. Michael watches over us on earth, a warrior ready for battle. He stands guard as God's sword.

Take your battles and struggles and place them in his guardianship. Entrust them to him, and he will aid and fight for you.

ST. MICHAEL, THE ARCH ANGEL, PRAY FOR US!

<u>Prayer to St. Michael the Archangel</u>

*Holy saint Michael, the Archangel, defend
us in battle.
Be our safeguard against the wickedness
and snares of the devil.
May God rebuke him, we humbly pray;
and do you,
O Prince of the heavenly host,
by the power of God cast into hell Satan and
all the evil spirits
who wander through the world seeking the
ruin of souls.
Amen.*

St. Raphael

St. Raphael is a wonderful archangel and a dear friend to me. I have come to rely upon him greatly.

As the Medicine of God, I have turned to him regularly for my chronic illness, relationships, and other important prayer requests.

St. Raphael has helped heal many and is a guide in times of darkness. He brings us closer to our loved ones and helps us find spouses and partners.

Like St. Raphael aided the young Tobias, he will aid us.

He has helped many in their relationships and struggles. He aids those struggling with illnesses. He soothes those in pain. He is the Lord's balm, healer, mender, and comforter.

Bring your plights to him, ask his intercession. Entrust your relationships, love life, pains, and illness to him. He is a reliable friend and angel.

ST. RAPHAEL, HEALER, AND GUIDE PRAY FOR US!

Prayer to Saint Raphael the Archangel.

Glorious Archangel Saint Raphael, great prince of the heavenly court, you are illustrious, for your gifts of wisdom and grace.
You are a guide of those who journey by land or sea or air, counselor of the afflicted and refuge of the sinners.
I beg you, assist me in all my needs and in all the sufferings of this life, as once you help the young Tobias on his travels, because you are the "medicine of God." I humbly pray you to heal the many infirmities of my soul and the ills that affect my body.
I especially ask you the favor.
(Mention your intention),
and the great grace of purity to prepare me to be the temple of the Holy Spirit.
Amen.

19 HOME

The yellow-washed church with a green tin roof. When I was growing up, this little church was a sign of home. Our Home was just around the corner whenever you could see the church.

The little church has stood there for a long time, longer than I have been alive— the cemetery on the corner where I grew up with the yellow church.

The church is a sign of home. Just as the feeling one gets when entering a Catholic Church, the feeling of home.

The Church and arms of Christ are our home on earth until we find our way to heaven after our last breaths.

God calls us in diverse ways, the biggest of which are His calls to home in Heaven and to serve.

There are times we will feel that call, the tug of the Church and the Holy Spirit speaking to our hearts and bidding us to draw closer to Christ to the Church.

Home can be more than a place and more than a feeling. It can be found in people and in prayer. Home can be a sense of belonging and can be wrapped up in many things.

A little church in the countryside has always been a place to call home—a sign that some things never change while others are constantly changing.

For us Catholics, the Church will always be a place to call home on this earth until we are called home to Heaven.

ST. ANTHONY'S CHURCH.

"He is preparing an eternal place for you." (John 14:2-4).

20 ANSWER KEEPER

"I am the Light of the world." (John 8:12).

Her heart was a beacon of Joy, and she radiated gratitude. She was a helping hand, a kindness found in the strangest of places. She was bright and warm, an example meant to reflect Christ.

There is a Light Within Me that draws others to me and yet is not my own. It is a glimpse of something and someone greater. I am only a girl, traveling the world searching for my purpose. Come with me. I will tell you of the light and where you, too, shall find it, for it is a light for all to find, one that is meant for the many and not only for the few. It does not keep time, for it is timeless. The Keeper of the Answers is not for me to keep alone but to share with all.

The light of Christ is the light; He is our guide, and He is the answer keeper.

Life can be filled with moments of searching and darkness. Yet there is always light. We can hold the answer and treasure that is found within the light within us.

Christ's light is within us, and he is the world's light. He is the answer keeper; looking inside, we can find that light. A light that shines bright in the darkest of times.

Life can be hectic and extremely busy, so remember to stop and take time to pray. For a minute, that is all you need. It does not have to be a complex prayer. It could simply be to thank God for all you have today.

ANNECY, FRANCE 2008.
"Thy Word is a lamp unto my feet and a light unto my path." Psalm 119;105
May you light candles and say a prayer at whatever church you visit in your journey in life.

21 HEALING WOUNDS

"Therefore, we do not lose heart. Though outwardly, we are wasting away; inwardly, we are being renewed day by day. For our light and momentary troubles are achieving for us an eternal glory that far outweighs them all." (2 Corinthians 4:16-18).

They say time heals all wounds.

However, they do not say what shape that will leave you in or how you will change afterward.

Time does heal all wounds, but nature steadies the mind and speaks to the soul.

Nature is an excellent place to return to when we need to heal, and time does not speak.

Heal ourselves by returning to that which we all come from, earth and land, nature itself.

The Lord heals the brokenhearted. He will mend the weary soul. Seek the Lord, and you will have all that you need.

Some wounds can take a long time to heal, and others, if left untreated, can fester.

He was wounded upon the cross and died for us. Bring your wounds to the healer.

Place yourself at the foot of the cross. Here, you will find healing and peace.

I have found that the Lord never gives me more than I can bear.

Though some days or moments are harder, or we struggle even more, whenever we look back, we can always see where God was working, which we could not at that moment in time.

Healing souls takes time, mending the broken heart and changing one's life trajectory.

It is all a part of a larger, grander plan, like a puzzle. We are slowly recognizing where all the pieces go.

"Heal me, Lord, and I will be healed; save me, and I will be saved, for you are the one I praise." (Jeremiah 17:14).

22 HE HEARS

"Don't spend your energies on things that generate worry, anxiety, and anguish. Only one thing is necessary: Lift up your spirit and love God."
Saint Padre Pio.

He hears our prayers, whether spoken or whispered, in our hearts and minds.

Prayer may not seem easy, but it is as simple as a positive thought or as simply saying thank you, Lord.

Prayers can be from a prayer card or straight from the heart.

We can often struggle with our prayer lives, and that is normal. Finding the time to pray in this current world can be difficult.

Remember that prayer can be many things.

Prayer is powerful, and we may not see its effects right away, but when the time comes, we will see all the changes it makes to our lives.

Maybe you don't know where to start in a prayer life, and my advice is to ask the Lord to help you let the Lord into your life.

Prayer is amazing, and so much good can come from it.

We may not always get the answer we seek, see a change, or feel any difference, but sometimes, God is just waiting for the right moment to change our lives and help us become the best we can be.

Prayer is not just a routine; it is a powerful connection to God.

In moments of joy and despair, let your prayers be a bridge to God's grace.

Pray fervently, whether in solitude or in the company of others, for in every prayer, you strengthen your bond with the Almighty.

He hears. Never forget that He hears.

23 ALONE

"I can do all things through Christ who strengthens me." (Philippians 4:13).

We do not have to do it all alone. The Lord is with us, and with him, we can do so much more.

May the light of the Lord shine in you today and help you to grow and come to know him better.

Have trust in the Lord and ask him for the strength you need.

God's grace is sufficient for us each day. Instead of worrying about the future, focus on the present moment.

Live today to the fullest, doing your best in all that you do.

Remember, God loves you just as you are, and it is time for you to love yourself too.

God has made us all; to him, we are beautiful despite whatever anyone says to us.

As long as we accept ourselves, we will always be loved by the Lord, even if we fail and mess up. The Lord has Mercy for us and forgives us. All we must do is ask. The Lord will give us the help we need. Do not try to do it all on your own because you are not alone.

Pray, pray, pray; you may not always get an answer right away or one at all. Trust in the Lord and his plan. Good things come to those who wait.

Lord, help us remember that nothing in our lives happens without your knowledge. Please help us to remember that you are always with us.

Amen.

24 A FRIEND FOR LIFE

Friends are always such a gift and blessing. I must say that in my short 26 years of life, I have been blessed with many amazing friends.

Sometimes, our friends are only in our lives for a short while, others a moment, and others a lifetime. What is a friend for life?

I suppose it is a friend who has been with us our whole life. Or, just maybe, it is that friend who, even when they are gone, a part of them remains with us.

I can say for certain that I have one friend in life who is like that. Who even after death still holds my hand still is a part of me even though he is gone.

When I was growing up, there was a certain routine to things. Somethings that could be relied upon.

We went to Sunday morning mass almost every week unless we had gone on a Saturday. Without fail, for as long as I can remember, people have always had their spots and places.

That is the thing about growing up in small towns. One tends to know everyone. Church was no exception. I remember he used to sit in the row behind us. One day, he started sitting in the pew with us.

I cannot remember exactly when. But I remember it was usual for my family to arrive and for him to be waiting at the end of the pew or for the spot to be left waiting for him to arrive. He was a widower his wife had passed away.

Yet he had always been a welcome fixture of the church. I do not remember when it started, but he started giving out jellybeans at church one day.

He was like another grandfather to me but also became my dearest friend.

He would slip us jellybeans as though a secret handshake during the sign of peace. He brought so much joy into one's life.

He had such a beautiful smile and soul.

I was twelve, turning thirteen, when Rudy passed away. Sometimes, I wonder if we were also close because our names were so close.

Just a letter flipped one way, and you would have his name and the other mine.

I think of him often.

Every Sunday, without fail, when it comes time to pray the Our Father, he comes to mind. I can see him smiling and remember he would squeeze my hand at the end of the prayer, like his own way of saying so many things.

Gone but never forgotten. I learned so much from him. I also learned more about death and loss from him.

Life can change so fast, and we should not take things for granted. We should be grateful for every minute.

It was not easy, and I missed him dearly. However, moving to a new town and not having to see the empty spot in the pew he used to sit in made it easier.

I learned about grief and how loss and sadness can mingle together in such a way. That even with so much time that has passed.

13 years this year since he died, and there are times I really miss him so much. Yet so many things bring him to mind and bring a smile to my face.

Rudy passed away, and, in many ways, I lost a very dear friend who gave me a love for Jellybeans and a great love for prayer cards stuffed in prayer books.

He left a lasting impact, and while he is no longer on this earth, my dearest friend, he will always be until my last breath.

Our Friendship will remain in my life. One day, I will see him again, and it will be the sweetest of things in the promise found in Heaven.

Rudy Dupilka was a radiant light, shining with such love and kindness. I wish more people were like him.

<u>Letters/notes from Rudy</u>

June 2009
'I want you to be my friend forever; I love you. May God Bless You.
Rudy."

June 2009
"Happy Birthday Ruby
Remember when I sat with you? We got to be friends, and now you are growing up to be a nice girl."
Rudy.

December 2009
"Merry Christmas and a Happy New Year to a nice friend like you. May God Bless you now and Forever, Ruby. I love You.
Rudy."

For Rudy, my friend, forever until I am old, and hair greyed, and memories faded until the day I return to the Father in Heaven where You will be waiting for me till we meet again, dear friend.

I believe everyone should meet someone like Rudy at least once in their lives.

I hope this short story reminds you that the smallest things can make the biggest impact.

REMEMBER THAT LIFE IS SHORT, SO ENJOY THE JELLYBEANS AND SMILE AT STRANGERS.

25 JELLYBEANS

There once was an old man whom
children loved.
He prayed often and brought smiles to
many a face.
He carried a worn-out prayerbook page
stuffed with prayer cards.
He would bring joy to all whom he
encountered.
He kept a secret tucked away.
Only those who were kind and
approached him with admiration could
receive this secret.
The secret of kindness is that anyone can
have it.
I learned kindness from a man with a
pocket full of beans, not just any beans but
jellybeans.
He was kind and sweet, just like the treat
he carried tucked away in his pockets, ready
and waiting to bring a smile to one's face.
He showed me that a little sweetness can
go a long way, and it moves the hearts of all
who receive but a few jellybeans.

26 THREE ANGELS

We do not always get the answers we need or want. Sometimes, we do not get to understand things, and it can be hard to comprehend.

Yet despite all this, the promise that it will all be revealed when one reaches heaven helps us move forward.

Growing up with four brothers and being the only girl, I always wanted a sister.

As much as I love each of my brothers, being the only girl could be extremely hard.

My family has been blessed with five of us children. While I was too little to remember the first miscarriage my mother had, I remember the other two times she was pregnant and miscarried.

Our three little angels in Heaven.

For whatever reason, God called them home before they could take their first breath. I wondered why, often, God had called them home, so soon I wondered why we did lose these siblings.

I remember praying and praying for a sister, and though my prayer was answered,

I never got to meet her.

Our three little angels are Emmaus, Isaiah, and Lily.

It might sound strange. However, I always talked to them in my prayers even though I could not hear it from them or know if they could even hear me.

I told them of our family and what we were doing or the prayer intentions I had, or the family had. I had asked them to pray with me.

Specifically, my sister Lily, as I was sure of her being with two of her brothers, she understood what it felt like to be outnumbered.

My siblings—there are eight of us in all. While I do not talk about them to many people, I always think about eight, not five, when I tell people how many siblings I have.

There was a time in my life after Rudy had died, and it was hard to process and understand what was happening within my heart.

It was the first real experience I had had with death and loss.

Even though I had lost my siblings, it was a different type of loss.

I remember talking to Lily a lot more that year. I remember praying and asking for a sign, something to help reassure me.

I remember asking Lily to help me know if it would be okay and how to make peace with the grief and loss I was feeling.

She was my little sister, my Angel. She heard my plea, at least that is what I like to believe, and she took it to Christ for me.

The next night, I had a dream, and it was a God Moment.

All I know is that after that, it was easier to work through the grief because I knew it would be okay, and I wanted to get to heaven even more.

I suppose this desire for heaven grew, as did the desire to know if it was a dream and just that or if it was something more.

27 A DREAM

I stand in a white flowing gown. I hear a choir singing and harps playing.

The cold path my bare feet walk softly on is made of sand.

Children are laughing in the distance, and I can see a garden with a throne room fit for a king.

I start to twirl and spin my feet, dancing, and then I see the choir.

They are angels, and they glow as they sing and play.

I asked a little boy who I did not know or recognize where I was.

He smiled at me and said I want to show you something.

I nodded, and he took my hand. We walked down a smaller path until we came to a wall.

He pointed, and I walked forward, leaned over, and looked down. I could see down far and wide, spreading out all the people I knew and strangers.

I saw different cities and towns everywhere; it changed as though a magical mirror was in front of me.

I looked back at the boy and asked, "Is that earth? Is this heaven? He smiled and nodded. He said there was more of this place to see, and I took his hand and followed him.

We went into a church and then came out into another garden filled with all kinds of people.

They were all the people I knew, and some I did not.

There were people there that I knew or who were family or friends.

Rudy was there, and so was my great-grandmother Katherine, who had died before I was born.

Other people were there that I recognized from pictures or from stories I heard growing up.

Children were playing, but three kids—two boys, one girl, and a dog—stood out to me.

I was not sure why my heart was so happy to see them until I heard them calling out each other's names.

My Grandma was knitting, the kids were playing, and Rudy was talking to his wife. I knew it was her even though I had never met her.

He was so happy to see me that he hugged me, and we talked for a while.

Rudy told me he loved me, and I told him I loved him too.

How much I missed him. He told me not to worry, that it would all be well.

After a while, one of the boys fell and cried.

My grandma then went and comforted him. She made it all better. I smiled, knowing my siblings were in such capable hands.

The children were playing with a ball. The little girl looked at me, smiled, and asked if I wanted to play.

I played with my siblings. It felt like I already knew them.

Later, I sat drawing them, trying to capture them while they played, hoping they would be engraved in my mind.

The little boy appeared again and told me it was time for me to leave, but not to worry, for when it was my time, I would join them in the garden.

When I woke up, I did not miss Rudy as

much; I loved him so much.

While I still missed him, I knew he was where he needed to be.

I knew if there were jellybeans in Heaven, he would be sure my siblings would get some.

I also knew then that my siblings were up there waiting for me.

I do not know the role of the little boy or why he was chosen to guide me. I like to think he will have a role I will learn about one day when I reach Heaven.

While I cannot say for certain that it was not all just a beautiful dream in a time of grief and loss, I also cannot say that it was not a glimpse of Heaven.

28 THANKSGIVING POEM

The Lord has given us the gift of life.
He will give us all that we need.
Always believe in the impossible.
Never lose hope, for if we have faith, we
have hope.
No, the Lord is always watching over you.
Stand strong, for he has great plans for you.
Give you praise, the Lord, and you shall
be blessed.
In darkness, we fight evil to bring light to
the world.
Valiant people protect the land from evil.
I am thankful for all who love and care for
me.
Nothing is stronger than the Lord, who
always watches.
God is fighting in a lengthy battle and
triumphs over evil.

29 FRIENDSHIPS

The Lord has blessed us with friendship.
He, too, knows the joys of earthly
friendships and how our friends can hold a
special place in our hearts.
Lord, thank you for the gift of friendship.
You yourself know the gifts of friendship.
You experienced them with the apostles
and in your friendships with Martha, Mary,
Lazarus, and John.
For my friends, though some were only
for a season and others a lifetime, all have
been important parts of my life.
Thank you for blessing me and my life,
my friends and their families and their
needs, and for protecting them. Amen.
The Lord understands the need for
friendship with people who will support us
in life's trials and hardships.
Remember to take time to thank him for
those friendships and the moments we
share with our friends.

<u>Prayer for friends.</u>

*Lord Jesus Christ, while on earth
You had close and devoted friends such
as John, Lazarus, Martha, and Mary.
You showed in this way that friendship is
one of the greatest blessings.
Thank you for the friends that You have
given me, in spite of my failures and
weaknesses, and to rich my life after Your
example.
Let me ever be behaved toward them, as
You behave towards your friends.
Bind us close together in You and enable
us to help one another on our Earthly
journey.
Amen.*

30 MY FRIENDS, THE SAINTS

My friends, the Saints, are always such an inspiration. There is a saint for almost everything, and I am always excited to learn about a new saint.

While I believe all saints are role models and have much to teach us. I have my favorites who have taught me a great deal firsthand.

Saints can teach us a great deal about faith, hardships, dealing with temptations, and living a Christ-centered life.

While we do not meet them until we reach Heaven, they have left us with directions and reminders.

They serve as role models and examples of faith, and through them, we can draw closer to Christ and the path to Heaven.

I have already introduced you to St. Giana and will introduce you to many more in this book; however, let me tell you how some of these other friendships began.

As there is more than one way to be introduced to a saint and become friends with them.

There are endless saints one can learn about, all with diverse backgrounds and patron saints for different needs or purposes.

I learned about some saints as I was growing up and through church, and others I discovered through a specific practice I like to follow.

I have always liked learning about saints, as there are so many, and sometimes, the saints had experiences or circumstances similar to ours that they had to overcome.

As I was growing up, my mom practiced adopting a saint for the year. At the beginning of the year, one picks a saint; throughout the year, one learns all about that Saint, grows to understand more about them, and, in some cases, becomes friends.

I started adopting saints for years; sometimes, I would choose them, and other times, they would choose me.

It is always exciting when I can find a Saint medal to add to my collection after finding a Saint.

One can also call it dedicating the year to a Saint. Just as sometimes the Pope declares a year to be for mercy or some other virtue, we ourselves can dedicate a year to a saint to pray to, learn about, and share with others.

Adopting a saint is a beautiful practice. Nowadays, there is even a saint generator that helps one choose a saint to adopt and get to know for the year.

Though we say it is just a year, it is amazing how that saint we adopt comes to have a bigger role in our lives. It becomes more than just a year as we develop a connection and form a sort of friendship with the saints.

So, I invite you to try adopting a saint for a year and see how God leads and inspires you through the life of the saint you choose.

The little moments with that saint will create a ripple effect in your life, and in the end, you will have a newfound friend for life.

A COLLECTION OF MY FRIENDS THE SAINT'S MEDALS.

31 THE FINDER OF LOST THINGS

There is a man, a keeper of lost things, one who is called upon in times of need. His name is Anthony, and he is the trusted keeper. Without fail and doubt, he will help you find whatever you are looking for.

One needs only to ask or say Tony, Tony, hurry, scurry. Anthony is the one to call upon, and he is my trusted friend and keeper of the missing things of things left somewhere and forgotten or misplaced—a finder of lost things and a friend to lost people.

Anthony, my dearest friend, thank you for always being such a reliable friend and keeping the lost in your heart.

St. Anthony is the Patron of Lost Things. Car keys, misplaced items, and things seemed to be lost and beyond the possibility of being found.

Remember to ask his intercession for lost things and unique needs as well.

Here is one of my favorite prayers.

"O blessed St. Anthony, The grace of God has made you a powerful advocate in all our needs and the patron for the restoration of things lost or stolen. I turn to you today with childlike love and deep confidence. You have helped countless children of God to find the things they have lost, material things, and, more importantly, The things of the spirit: faith, hope, and love. I come to you with confidence; help me with my present need. I recommend what I have lost to your care, In the hope that God will restore it to me, If it is His holy Will.
Amen."

While I have made friends with many Saints over the years, I always say Saint Anthony found me. I was choosing a saint for the year, and I could not decide which Saints, so I prayed for guidance. Days later, everywhere I looked, I found prayers, saint medals, novenas, all Saint Anthony of Padua emerging. I like to think he chose me. I was lost, and he found me. He is the keeper of lost things.

He has become a reliable source for praying for things lost and for things for which I am searching.

Saint Anthony is a reliable saint to pray to, whether for a petition or for a specific need. Prayers are in good hands when placed in his hands.

When one needs direction, a course of action, or a sign, ask Saint Anthony. I like to think of petitioning St. Anthony as when one is lost and asks for directions.

A weary traveler approaches one with their worries, and they petition, asking for directions.

Who is better than the patron saint of lost things to give one direction about one's life?

So, turn to the Saint of lost things and ask for directions in your life, directions on things you are concerned about, and directions on being directionless. Trust him to guide and aid you; he will intercede for you.

If we think about it, lost things are important to God.

We think of the lost sheep parable in Matthew; even if a man has one hundred sheep and one wanders away, he leaves the ninety-nine to search for that one lost. It is fitting that God would give a Saint the gift of finding lost things.

so that we, too, could find lost things, so that we could be found when we are lost.

ST. ANTHONY, PRAY FOR US!

<u>Unfailing Prayer to Saint Anthony</u>.

*O Holy St. Anthony, gentlest of saints,
your love for God and charity for His
creatures.
Made you worthy, when on earth to
possess miraculous powers.
Miracles waited on your word, which you
were ever ready to speak for those in
trouble or anxiety.
Encouraged by this thought, I implore of
you to obtain for me.
(Request.)
The answer to my prayer may require a
miracle, even though you are the Saint of
miracles.
O gentle and loving, Saint Anthony,
whose heart was ever so full of human
sympathy,
whisper my petition into the ears of the
sweet infant Jesus,
who loved to be folded in your arms, and
gratitude of my heart will be ever yours.
Amen.*

32 HE REMAINS

She had been praying for a miracle. She had a list of prayers and countered blessings. She wondered how he could use her sufferings, how her story would be told, and if others would be able to see him within it. What details would stay within people's minds? She longed to share his goodness, for there to be light until the end of her days, for there to be light until the end of her days, for there to be light until the end of her days, for her to live life with a grateful heart and love overflowing. There were moments of wounding ever so deep, days filled with pain and agony. Yet he remained by her side. He soothed her soul and brought hope. Even in the darkest times, there was strength within the weakness and mercy within the confusion and doubt. He held her hand when no one else could see the pain. By her side, he shall remain.

33 ST. RITA

Saint Rita had a deep desire as a child to become a nun. However, she married as they desired her to out of obedience and respect for her parents. She was a wife and mother dedicated to her faith. Her husband was abusive, and she suffered greatly yet offered up her sufferings. After her sons and husband died, she finally joined the sisters. She became known as a holy and prayerful nun for her meditation and prayer before the crucifixion.

Saint Rita of Cascia is a saint known for the impossible now, saying that having the impossible intercessor is always a good friend to have. She has helped me through some really difficult times in my life, with her suffering bearing the thorn inside her forehead and following the Holy Spirit. Her faith in Christ was unshakable.

While I have not visited her resting place and convent in Cascia, I will one day. I suppose I have a deal with Saint Rita.

<u>Petition Prayer</u>

*O Powerful St. Rita,
rightly called Saint of the Impossible,
I come to you with confidence in my great
need.
You know well my trials,
for you yourself were many times burdened
in this life.
Come to my help, speak for me, pray with
me,
intercede on my behalf before the Father.
I know that God has a most generous heart
and that he is a most loving Father.
Join your prayers to mine
and obtain for me the grace I desire:
(Share your request...)
You who were so very pleasing to God on
earth
and are so much more now in heaven,
I promise to use this favor when granted,
to better my life, to proclaim God's mercy,
and to make you more widely known and
loved.
Amen.*

ST. RITA OF CASCIA, PRAY FOR US!

St. Rita Prayer of Intercession

Glorious St. Rita, O Holy Patroness of those in need, your intercession with our Lord is most powerful. Through the favors obtained by your prayers, you have been called the Advocate of the Hopeless and even of the Impossible. St. Rita, humble and pure; patient and compassionate lover of Christ Crucified! We have confidence that everyone who has recourse to you, will find comfort and relief. Listen to our petitions and show your power with God on our behalf. Obtain our petitions for us, if they are for the greater glory of God, and for our good. We promise if our petitions are granted, to make known your favor and to glorify God for His gift. Relying on your merits and power before the Sacred Heart of Jesus, we ask of you: (Share your request...)
Obtain for us our request:
– by the singular merits of your childhood,
– by your perfect union with the Divine Will,
– by your heroic sufferings during your married life,

– by the consolation you experienced at the
conversion of your husband,
– by the sacrifice of your children rather
than see them grievously offend God,
– by your miraculous entrance into the
convent,
– by your severe penances and thrice daily
bloody scourging,
– by the suffering caused by the wound you
received from the thorn of the Crucified
Savior,
– by the divine love which consumed your
heart,
– by that remarkable devotion to the
Blessed Sacrament, on which alone you
existed for four years,
– by the happiness with which you parted
from your trials to join your Divine Spouse,
– by the perfect example you gave to people
of every state of life.
Pray for us, O Holy St. Rita, that we may
be made worthy of the promises of Christ.
Let us Pray: Heavenly Father, in Your
infinite love and mercy, you heed the prayer
of Your beloved servant, Saint Rita. You
graciously grant favors through her
intercession, which are considered

impossible to human foresight, skill, and efforts. Relying on her compassionate love, we ask You to assist us in our trials and difficulties. Let unbelievers know that you are the helper of the humble, the defense of the helpless, and the strength of those who trust in You. We ask this through Jesus Christ our Lord. Amen.

34 ST. JUDE

They say Saint Jude Thaddeus can often be forgotten because of the other Jude and his betrayal of Christ.

Saint Jude Thaddeus deals with impossible or difficult circumstances. He is the Patron of hopeless causes.

He is such a trusted saint that I petition him for the big and important things as well as the small things.

Thaddeus means generous, kind, and courageous. The Lord said He will show himself most willing to help.

There are so many reasons to turn to St. Jude and ask for his aid.

I have found great help in all sorts of circumstances, and St. Jude has become the dearest friend to me.

St. Jude's Feast Day is on October 28th. St. Jude is often depicted with a flame above his head, signifying his presence at Pentecost. He is most often seen holding an image of Christ on a metal.

Prayer to St. Jude

St. Jude, glorious Apostle,
faithful servant and friend of Jesus, the
name of the traitor has caused you to be
forgotten by many, but the true Church
invokes you universally as the Patron of
things despaired of: pray for me, who am so
miserable;
pray for me, that finally I may receive the
consolations and the succor of Heaven in all
my necessities, tribulations, and sufferings,
particularly.
(here make your request),
and that I may bless God with the Elect
throughout Eternity.
Amen.

St. Jude Novena

*"Apostle and Martyr, great in virtue and
rich in miracles,
near kinsman of Jesus Christ, faithful
intercessor for all who invoke thee,
special patron in time of need; to thee I
have recourse from the depth of my heart,
and humbly beg thee,
to whom God hath given such great
power, to come to my assistance;
help me now in my urgent need and
grant my earnest petition.
I will never forget thy graces and the
favors thou dost obtain for me, and I will do
my utmost to spread devotion to thee.
Amen."*

ST. JUDE, PRAY FOR US

35 ST. CLARE

"Our labor here is brief, but the reward is eternal. Do not be disturbed by the clamor of the world, which passes like a shadow. Do not let false delights of a deceptive world deceive you." St. Clare of Assisi.

St. Clare was Friends with St. Francis, and her friend's teachings inspired her. She had such a deep faith. She started the monastic religious order for women, the Order of Poor Ladies, which became the Poor Clare Sisters.

St. Clare came from a wealthier family in Assisi and turned away from wealth and embraced poverty.

She wrote the Rule of Life, which became the guidelines for the poor Clare monastery and sisters that followed her.

St. Clare was deeply dedicated to the Holy Eucharist and loved Christ in the Holy Sacrament of the Mass.

Through her example, Eucharistic adoration has taken on an even deeper meaning for me.

ST. CLARE, PRAY FOR US!

"Love Him Totally who gave Himself totally for your love." St. Clare.

Prayer for Healing

O Blessed Saint Clare,
your life shines like a beacon
and cast its light down the ages of the
Church
to guide the way of Christ.
Look with compassion on the poor and
humble
who call on you for help.
As you bow before your Eucharistic Lord in
Heaven,
speak to Him of my afflicted body and my
broken spirit.
Ask Him to heal me and to wash away my
sins
in His precious Blood.
Great Servant of Christ,
remember the needs of my family
and all those I pray for.
Defend us from everything
that would threaten our Holy Catholic faith.
Hear the cry of the poor
and make it a song of intercession,
rising from your poor heart
to the Eucharistic Heart of Jesus, our Healer,
our Savior, and our Lord. Amen.

Prayer to St. Clare

*O Glorious St. Clare,
God has given you the power of working
miracles continually,
and the favor of answering the prayers
of those who invoke your assistance in
misfortune,
anxiety, and distress; we beseech you,
obtain for us from Jesus,
through Mary,
His Blessed Mother,
what we beg of you so fervently and
hopefully,
if it be for the greater honor and glory of
God and for the good of our souls.
Amen.
Saint Clare: Pray For Us.*

36 THE POOR CLARE'S

The Poor Clare's are cloistered nuns. This means they do not leave its grounds once they enter the monastic convent.

I met the Poor Clare sisters in 2010 when I first visited their cloistered monastery in Mission, BC. The Convent Monastery is just down the road from Westminster Abbey.

Nestled in the hustle and bustle of the world, the Monastery is beautiful and cozy, set apart from the world.

Cloistered means that while guests can visit, they cannot enter the convent itself. There is a separate entrance for guests to come and speak to the sisters or visit their beautiful chapel. Bars separate the outside world. Monastic life is ever so beautiful.

They dedicate their lives to God and close themselves off from the world in a unique way, where one is focused on hearing and serving God and not the things of this world.

Since our meeting, the sisters and I have been pen pals, and I enjoy reading and receiving their newsletters, exchanging letters, praying intentions, and receiving spiritual encouragement.

Having spiritual sisters is essential, especially when one has all brothers. I turn to my sisters in times of need and joy. They are beautiful people who emanate the light and love of Christ, with a devotion to the Eucharist and poverty.

At one time, I also considered and discerned being a Poor Clare sister myself.

The Poor Clares live a beautiful life dedicated to Christ, poverty, and their mission.

The sisters have inspired me to live simply and humbly and given me an appreciation for living with less.

I want to be less focused on the world and physical things. Because when we die, all the things of this earth will stay here, and Our souls and spirits go to Heaven, leaving this earthly home and possessions behind.

So, I encourage you to learn more about religious life. If you are interested in learning more about the Poor Clare sisters, please visit their website.
https://poorclare.ca/

"We become what we love, and who we love shapes what we become. If we love things, we become a thing. If we love nothing, we become nothing. Imitation is not a literal mimicking of Christ, rather it means becoming the image of the beloved, an image disclosed through transformation. This means we are to become vessels of God's compassionate love for others." St. Clare of Assisi.

Prayer to Saint Clare

*God of Mercy, you inspired St. Clare with
the love of poverty.
By the help of her prayers, may we follow
Christ in poverty of spirit and come to the
joyful vision of Your glory in the Kingdom of
heaven.
We ask this through our Lord Jesus Christ,
your Son, who lives and reigns with you and
the Holy Spirit, one God, forever and ever.
Amen.*

Eucharistic prayer

*O Blessed Saint Clare, your life shines like
a beacon and cast its light down the ages of
the Church to guide the way of Christ.
Look with compassion on the poor and
humble who call on you for help.
As you bow before your Eucharistic Lord
in Heaven, speak to Him of my afflicted
body and my broken spirit.
Amen.*

37 ST. FRANCIS OF ASSISI

"Start by doing what is necessary, then what is possible, and suddenly you are doing the impossible." St. Francis of Assisi.

St. Francis of Assisi is known as the patron saint of Italy and of Animals.

He was born into a wealthy family, but once he devoted his life to God, he took on the name Francis, relinquishing all ties to his past life.

He was a wild young man and was supposed to set out to war when illness struck.

He heard God in prayer in his illness and knew he needed to change his ways. His father disowned him after he tried to give away wealth and help the poor.

He heard God speak to him, telling him to go and build up his house and church. He rebuilt the church and then devoted his life to prayer, sharing the gospel, and his mission of poverty.

He gathered followers and founded the

order of the Franciscans. He traveled preaching and bringing others closer to Christ. He was a mystic and a poet.

Today, he is a very well-known saint and is often quoted.

I have found such inspiration in St. Francis. He was also a good friend of St. Anthony, so we are in good company.

"Remember that when you leave this earth, you can take with you nothing that you have received - only what you have given: a full heart enriched by honest service, love, sacrifice, and courage." St. Francis of Assisi.

The Poor Clares and other Franciscan orders took on St. Francis's words, devoting their lives to poverty and service to God. St. Francis has left an example that has had a ripple effect in religious life and in the lives of regular people.

He teaches us to love for all and the creatures of this earth—a real role model to have in one's life.

<u>Saint Francis's Prayer Before the Blessed Sacrament</u>

We adore You,
O Lord Jesus Christ,
in this Church and all the Churches of the
world,
and we bless You,
because,
by Your holy Cross You have redeemed the
world. Amen.

<u>Saint Francis's Prayer Before the Crucifix</u>

Most High, glorious God,
enlighten the darkness of my heart and give
me
true faith, certain hope, and perfect charity,
sense and knowledge, Lord, that I may carry
out
Your holy and true command. Amen.

ST. FRANCIS, PRAY FOR US!

Prayer of St. Francis of Assisi (Prayer for Peace)

*Lord, make me an instrument of your
peace:
Where there is hatred, let me sow love;
Where there is injury, pardon;
Where there is doubt, faith;
Where there is despair, hope;
Where there is darkness, light;
where there is sadness, joy.
O divine Master, grant that I may not so
much seek.
to be consoled as to console,
to be understood as to understand,
To be loved as to love.
For it is in giving that we receive,
it is in pardoning that we are pardoned,
and it is in dying that we are born to eternal
life.
Amen.*

<u>Saint Francis's Canticle of All Creatures</u>

*Most High, all-powerful, all-good Lord, All
praise is Yours, all glory, all honor and all
blessings.
To you alone, Most High, do they belong,
and no mortal lips are worthy to pronounce
Your Name.
Praised be You my Lord, with all Your
creatures,
especially Sir Brother Sun,
Who is the day through whom You give us
light.
And he is beautiful and radiant with great
splendor,
Of You Most High, he bears the likeness.
Praised be You, my Lord, through Sister
Moon and the stars,
In the heavens, you have made them bright,
precious, and fair.
Amen.*

38 BURING BRIGHT

A burning love ever so bright.
I longed for a love that emulated Christ's love. I wonder if I will find one that is so true and if it exists.
Maybe it's just a fairy tale, yet I hope there is a love like that that exists for me.
I long to love Christ with complete love like that of the saints.
I am grateful to have such great devotion to him and the kingdom of Heaven as the inspirational men and women who have been guides and mentors to me in faith, hope, and truth.
Burning ever so bright is the love of Christ.
One can only pray and hope to grow to emulate the love Christ has for us. To find those who will help draw us closer to Christ through prayer and works.

39 ARMOR OF GOD

"Finally, be strong in the Lord and in his mighty power. Put on the full armor of God, so that you can take your stand against the devil's schemes. For our struggle is not against flesh and blood, but against the rulers, against the authorities, against the powers of this dark world and against the spiritual forces of evil in the heavenly realms. Therefore, put on the full armor of God, so that when the day of evil comes, you may be able to stand your ground, and after you have done everything, to stand. Stand firm then, with the belt of truth buckled around your waist, with the breastplate of righteousness in place, and with your feet fitted with the readiness that comes from the gospel of peace. In addition to all this, take up the shield of faith, with which you can extinguish all the flaming arrows of the evil one. Take the helmet of salvation and the sword of the Spirit, which is the word of God."
(Ephesians 6:10-17), NIV.

We should all strive to put on the armor of God at the beginning of each day.

My favorite saint to ask for aid in this is St. Joan of Arc, a girl who became a soldier for the Lord.

It is important to surround ourselves with things that protect us, strengthen us, and bring us closer to Christ. The armor of God does that and so much more.

We can also ask St. Michael, the Arch Angel, to assist us in putting on the armor of God.

<u>The Armor of God</u>

The Belt of Truth.
The Breastplate of Righteousness.
The Shoes of the Gospel of Peace.
The Shield of Faith.
The Helmet of Salvation.
The Sword of the Spirit: Word of God.

40 ST. JOAN OF ARC

It is better to be alone with God. His friendship will not fail me, nor His counsel, nor His love. In His strength, I will dare and dare and dare until I die—St. Joan of Arc.

While there are many amazing women Saints, Saint Joan of Arc was a soldier, a warrior, and a messenger of God. She had such courage and was dedicated to carrying out the mission God placed into her hands.

This French girl played a huge role in France's history of battle, and we should all strive to follow her example. Saint Joan of Arc played a role in insisting on Charles VII of France's coronation, which took place during the one hundred years of war. She was guided by St. Michael and a couple of other saints in her quest to help protect France from the English.

This was after God spoke to her and told her what needed to be done for France to succeed.

She was Martyred and burned at the stake for her faith and for following Christ.

If I ever Have to go into a spiritual battle with the devil. She would be the first to be at my side. I come to her whenever I need to be brave.

She had such courage and was dedicated to carrying out the mission God had placed in her hands.

St. Joan of Arc was seventeen years old when she started her quest. She became a soldier, and by age 19, she was captured and put to death for being accused of heresy by the English. Later, this conviction was overturned, and her name restored, but not till after she was burned alive.

St. Joan of Arc has inspired many other saints. During the time, women soldiers were not approved of, and she caused a stir.

She is a beautiful example of following Christ and being willing to die for her faith and beliefs. She was a devoted catholic and protector of France.

So, when you are struggling, afraid, or trying to battle the devil, turn to this trusty saint.

ST. JOAN OF ARC, PRAY FOR US!

"I am not afraid; I was born to do this." St. Joan of Arc.

<u>Prayer to Saint Joan of Arc</u>

In the face of your enemies,
In the face of harassment, ridicule, and
doubt, you held firm in your faith.
Even in your abandonment, alone and
without friends, you held firm in your faith.
Even as you faced your own mortality, you
held firm in your faith.
I pray that I may be as bold.
In my beliefs as you, St. Joan.
I ask that you ride alongside me.
In my own battles.
Help me be mindful that what is
Worthwhile can be won when I persist.
Help me hold firm in my faith.
Help me believe in my ability.
To act well and wisely.
Amen.

Novena to Saint Joan of Arc.

*Glorious Saint Joan of Arc,
filled with compassion for those who
invoke you,
with the love for those who suffer heavily
laden with the weight of my troubles,
I kneel at your feet and humbly beg you
to take my present knee under your special
protection.
(Mention Request here.)
Vouchsafe to recommend it to the
Blessed Virgin Mary and lay it before the
throne of Jesus.
Cease not to intercede for me, until my
request is granted.
Above all obtained from me the grace to
one day meet God face to face, and with
you and Mary and all the angels and Saints.
Praise Him through all eternity.
O most powerful Saint Joan of Arc, do
not let me lose my soul, but obtain for me
the grace of winning my ways to heaven
forever and ever.
Amen.*

41 A ROSE WINDOW

The term rose window is a generic term often applied to a circular window, and in this case, it is related to Gothic cathedrals and churches.

These circular windows usually have their stained glass divided into segments or sections separated by tracery or stone mullions.

The Cathedral of Notre Dame has three rose windows, one in the West, one in the South, and one in the North. Each of these three rows of windows has its own color choices that best suit the light it receives at various times of the day. This is due to the separate times of restoration and cleaning, as well as to history and those who decided to update or change, particularly what was being shown.

The South rose window depicts Mother Mary holding Christ surrounded by kings and prophets from the Old Testament.

There is something moving and captivating about the Rose Window in the Notre Dame Cathedral; seeing it with one's own eyes is exciting.

I remember I felt ever so small in front of it—the colors of stained glass and all the stories it tells.

A window into faith. Handcrafted mosaic that glowed with breathtaking beauty

*NOTRE-DAME CATHEDRAL
PARIS, FRANCE 2008.*

ROSE WINDOW
NOTRE-DAME CATHEDRAL
PARIS, FRANCE 2008.

42 UNCEASING LOVE

His love for us is unending and unceasing.
It is comparable and sometimes
incomprehensible.
He loves us without conditions, and he
loves us as we are, our faults and our
weaknesses.
True love is the love of Christ; if you are
seeking love, seek out Christ.
The true source of love is Christ.
Place your heart into his hands and let
him guide you.
The Lord loves you, and we are all
children of God.

*"NEITHER HEIGHT NOR DEPTH,
NOR ANYTHING ELSE IN ALL
CREATION, WILL BE ABLE TO
SEPARATE US FROM THE LOVE OF
GOD THAT IS IN CHRIST JESUS OUR
LORD." (ROMANS 8:39).*

43 BASILICA OF THE VISITATION

It was one of those side trips that was a gift for us. At the time, my mom was learning about St. Jane Frances De Chantal. We did not know she and St. Francis De Sales would also be at the Basilica of the Visitation.

We had considered if the side trip would be worth it, and we decided it was.

God gives us moments these times where we can have inspiration and feel closer to him.

Both of these saints had a deep love and faith. They desired to serve God and live a life filled with poverty and purity.

He uses the Saints as mentors and teachers to help us along the way. These Saints are such an inspiration and have taught me how to learn and grow closer to Christ.

He gives us examples of faith to follow within the Saints.

BASILICA OF THE VISITATION.
ANNECY, FRANCE, 2008.

ST. FRANCIS DE SALES.

ST. JANE FRANCES DE CHANTAL.

THE PRAYER OF ST. FRANCIS DE SALES

*Be at peace.
Do not look forward in fear to the changes
of life;
rather look to them with full hope as they
arise.
God, whose very own you are, will deliver
you from out of them.
He has kept you hitherto, and He will lead
you safely through all things;
and when you cannot stand it, God will bury
you in his arms.
Do not fear what may happen tomorrow;
the same everlasting Father who cares for
you today
will take care of you then and every day.
He will either shield you from suffering, or
give you unfailing strength to bear it.
Be at peace, and put aside all anxious
thoughts and imagination.
Amen.*

PRAYER FOR INNER STRENGTH AND SERENITY

O glorious saint, blessed Jane Frances,
by fervent prayer, attention to the Divine Presence,
and purity of intention,
you attained on earth an intimate union with God.
Be now our advocate, our mother,
our guide in the path of virtue and perfection.
Plead our cause near Jesus, Mary, and Joseph,
to whom you were so tenderly devoted, and
whose holy virtues you so closely imitated.
Obtain for us, O amiable and compassionate Saint,
the virtues you deem most necessary for us;
an ardent love of Jesus in the most holy Sacrament,
a tender and filial confidence in His Blessed Mother,
and like you, a constant remembrance
of His sacred Passion and death.
Obtain also, we pray, that our particular
intention in this prayer may be granted.

Pray for us, O holy St. Jane Frances.
Amen.

"When shall it be that we shall taste the sweetness of the Divine Will in all that happens to us, considering in everything only His good pleasure, by whom it is certain that adversity is sent with as much love as prosperity, and as much for our good? When shall we cast ourselves undeservedly into the arms of our most loving Father in Heaven, leaving to Him the care of ourselves and of our affairs, and reserving only the desire of pleasing Him, and of serving Him well in all that we can?"

~

"Hold your eyes on God and leave the doing to him. That is all the doing you have to worry about." -St. Jane Frances de Chantal.

Letter to Saint Francis de Sales, from Saint Jane Frances de Chantal

"How soon may I hope for the happy day when I shall irrevocably offer myself to my God? He has so filled me with the thought of being entirely His, and it has come home to me in such a wonderful and powerful manner, that, were my emotion to last as it now is, I could not live under its intensity. Never have I had such a burning love and desire for the evangelical life and for the great perfection to which God calls me. What I feel about it is quite impossible to put into words.

But, alas! My resolve to be very faithful to the greatness of the love of this divine Savior is balanced by the feeling of my incapacity to correspond with it.

Oh, how painful to love is this barrier of powerlessness!

But why do I speak thus?

By doing so, I degrade, it seems to me, the gift of God which urges me to live in perfect poverty, in humble obedience, and in spotless purity.

44 THE LITTLE WAY

"Without love, deeds, even the most brilliant, count as nothing." — Thérèse de Lisieux.

Life can be filled with many big and exciting things. It is most often the little moments where the small things end up leaving the biggest impact, like that of a crayon drawing a simple thing yet causing a lasting ripple.

St. Thérèse and her little way encourages the small things, the little moments we can Offer Up to God and others. I learned from Saint Thérèse how her little way can be big things, all added up from the little things. She loved Our Lady deeply and sought to serve the Lord from an early age.

The Little Way is described as a way of approaching life and spirituality.

St. Thérèse said," *You must practice the little virtues.*"

I learned how to appreciate the little things and how the little things can become big things. All the little sins add up and, without confession, turn into big things.

"My little way is the way of spiritual childhood, the way of trust and absolute self-surrender." Thérèse of Lisieux.

ST. THÉRÈSE OF LISIEUX
LISIEUX FRANCE
JUNE 2008.

ST. THÉRÈSE OF LISIEUX, PRAY FOR US!

Novena Rose Prayer

*O Little Therese of the Child Jesus, please
pick for me a rose.
from the heavenly gardens and send it to
me as a message of love.
O Little Flower of Jesus, ask God to grant
the favors.
I now place confidence in your hands.
(mention in silence here)
St. Therese, help me to always believe as
you did in
God's great love for me, so that I might
imitate your "Little Way" each day.
Amen.*

Miraculous Invocation to St. Therese

*O Glorious St. Therese,
whom Almighty God has raised up to aid
and inspire the human family,
I implore your Miraculous Intercession.
You are so powerful in obtaining every
need.
of body and spirit from the Heart of God.
Holy Mother Church proclaims you "Prodigy
of Miracles...*

the greatest saint of Modern Times."
Now, I fervently beseech you to answer
my petition.
(mention in silence here)
and to carry out your promises of
spending heaven doing good on earth...
Of letting fall from Heaven a Shower of
Roses.
Little Flower, give me your childlike faith,
to see the Face of God
in the people and experiences of my life,
And to love God with full confidence.
St. Therese, my Carmelite Sister,
I will fulfill your plea "to be made known
everywhere."
And I will continue to lead others to Jesus
through you.
Amen.

**"Miss no single opportunity of making
some small sacrifice, here by a
smiling look, there by a kindly word;
always doing the smallest right and
doing it all for love." St. Thérèse de
Lisieux.**

BASILLICA OF ST. THÉRÈSE OF LISIEUX,2008.

ST. THÉRÈSE OF LISIEUX, FRANCE, 2008.

ST. THÉRÈSE OF LISIEUX RELIQUARY,
FRANCE, 2008.

ST. THÉRÈSE OF LISIEUX RELIQUARY,
FRANCE, 2008.

45 THE GRATEFUL HEART

"I give thanks to you, O Lord my God, with my whole heart, and I will glorify your name forever." (Psalm 86:12).

Gratitude comes in many forms.

A grateful heart can change one's day exponentially.

I learned that picking three things to be grateful for in a day, whether at the beginning or the end of the day, once one has three things, more follows.

I am grateful to God for every day, even the challenging and difficult ones.

There are so many things to be grateful for in this life.

I have been very blessed to have so many amazing people teaching me about gratitude and having an open heart.

I am so grateful for those who have impacted my life and have played a role in shaping me and my faith.

Within him, our hearts are made whole.

<u>A Prayer for a Grateful Heart</u>

Dearest Jesus, create in me a grateful heart. May I always give thanks to you, not just for the good but also in the difficult times.
May I be grateful for the opportunities to serve you and to seek your will.
Thank you for the gift of this day and all it will contain. Thanks be to God in all joy and sorrow. Thank you, Lord, for loving me even at my darkest.
Give thanks to the Lord. Rejoice and let our hearts be glad.
Thank the Lord for the things that bring you joy today. Thank him for the moments we feel his presence and for the moments we do not.
Lord, teach us to have a grateful heart. To love others as you love us.
Amen.

46 BLESSED

Life can be full of blessings—moments when lives are touched or filled with grace. The Lord blesses us in multiple ways.

We are blessed with God's merciful love and the gifts of the Holy Spirit.

While I have been blessed with many God moments, instances that have fueled my faith and kept me going, there have been times when it is a desert, and searching for God can be challenging, and darkness can come.

Since I was a teenager, I have been chronically ill.

It is my own cross and burden to bear.

While I do not draw too much attention to it, and to most people who do not know me well, it is hard to see that I am ill.

While God gives us beautiful things and experiences, he also gives us difficulties and challenges things to help teach us something important or to help us to be stronger; many times, it is to be able to persevere for something even harder that has yet to come into our lives.

The Lord has given us a path, instructions, and guidance. He tells us how we are blessed and prepares us for challenging times.

The Beatitudes (Matthew 5:1-12).

"Blessed are the poor in spirit, for theirs is the kingdom of heaven. Blessed are those who mourn, for they will be comforted. Blessed are the meek, for they will inherit the earth. Blessed are those who hunger and thirst after righteousness, for they will be filled. Blessed are the merciful, for they shall be shown mercy. Blessed are the pure in heart, for they will see God. Blessed are the peacemakers, for they will be called the sons of God. Blessed are those who are persecuted because of righteousness, for theirs is the kingdom of heaven. Blessed are you when people insult you, persecute you, and falsely say all kinds of evil against you because of me. Rejoice and be glad, because great is your reward in heaven, for in the same way they persecuted the prophets who were before you."

47 THE VOICE OF A SOUL

"Behold, I stand at the door and knock. If anyone hears My voice and opens the door, I will come into him and dine with him, and he with Me." *(Rev 3:20).*

They say the soul can speak. If our souls can speak, why is it so hard to discern the direction one needs to go?

Yet the truth is that we just forget how to listen to the voice of our souls. Our souls cry out. If you listen, you will feel and hear it.

There is a feeling that creeps in. It speaks to the heart, whispering its own secret language. Oh, how the heart is ever so fond these whispers in its absence beg for it seeks and desires it.

While our souls perhaps long for a soulmate, another half.

In a spiritual context, this 'soulmate' is not necessarily a romantic partner, but a spiritual companion, a connection with God that can make our souls completely whole.

Our souls yearn for Christ and his light. Christ can hear the cries of our souls and knows what we need before we can even comprehend our own needs.

Seeking Christ brings a profound sense of fulfillment and purpose.

Listen to the voice of your soul. Let it speak to you.

Search out for Christ, let him speak to your soul, and give you what you need.

The Voice of a Soul is like that of a bell tower that rings out, announcing the time or the beginning of mass. It is a call to our souls.

A call that announces the approach of Christ. Listen for the call. Listen to the voice of your soul.

If you cannot hear it, then visit your nearest church and let God speak to your soul.

Seek the Voice of God. Knock on the door.

WESTMINISTER ABBEY BELL TOWER,
MISSION, BC 2012.

48 Westminster Abey

"But as we go forward in our life and in faith, we shall with hearts enlarged and unspeakable sweetness of love run in the way of God's commandments."

– Rule of St. Benedict, Prologue.

Westminster Abbey, or Seminary of Christ the King, is a Benedictine Monastery. It is a community of monks who are committed to the order of St. Benedict as brothers or priests.

Westminster Abbey was founded in 1939 and is a thriving monastic community filled with men who have dedicated their lives to God.

I have learned so much about monastic life from the brothers and the monks.

My brothers attended the minor seminar, and I had the opportunity to gain more brothers and grow in faith while they were journeying and learning in school.

I learned to love the Liturgy of the Hours, the Benedictine Way, and the Rule of Saint Benedict.

The Rule of St. Benedict, a book written

by St. Benedict for the monks to follow, is a transformative guide. It describes the rules and practices of a monk and those of the Benedictine orders, which the monks follow and practice daily, leading to spiritual enlightenment and guidance.

Monastic life offers much to gain and learn from in the secular world.

The monastery shows how those of faith can live in a community, how simplicity can play a huge role in life, and how the mentality of less is more.

There is a story about a famous brother, Brother Lawrence, who discusses finding God amongst the pots and pans. Within the book *The Practice of the Presence of God*.

For many religious orders, prayer, and work go hand in hand, bringing us closer to God in both instances. In this instance, we can pray within our everyday tasks and be drawn closer to Christ.

The Latin phrase and motto for the Benedictine monks is Ora et Labora (Pray and Work). It is a part of their daily lives. Each day begins and ends with prayer.

The days are also filled with work. No job is too high or too low; all work is for the

Love of God and the community.

In our secular world, we cannot be as dedicated to prayer and God as those in the monastery.

They have created their own rhythm of life, which sets them apart.

We need to learn to pray through our work and tasks and find God with the piles of laundry and dishes during work hours and our daily commutes.

The Abbey is in Mission, BC, and is a full-time high school and major seminary.

It is a place for young men to grow in faith and discern the priesthood.

They also have a guesthouse where you can book a retreat. Benedictine monks also practice hospitality.

The monks are welcoming and open to conversation within their guest house or the grounds unless they are practicing monastic silence for a period to draw themselves closer to God.

Spending time with and speaking with the monks is very beneficial.

Their vocation is a gift and inspiration that reminds us that we are all called to be saints. It is like being welcomed into a loving family in Christ.

The monastery has a tall bell tower that rings out far and wide for all to hear. It is a heavenly and peaceful place, and I hope others take the time to enjoy it.

It is as though Christ is calling out to our souls and calling us home.

The boys and young men who go to school or seminary at the monastery live and work with the monks, embracing the monastic rules and practices of the Catholic faith and the rules of St. Benedict.

While there are many other Benedictine monks worldwide, this is the only Benedictine Seminary in Canada.

Perhaps other families will discover this beautiful place and have their sons attend.

I know I have gained some fantastic spiritual brothers while my brothers were attending seminary.

If you want to visit Westminster Abbey or learn more, please visit the website below.

https://westminsterabbey.ca/benedictine-monasticism/

WESTMINSTER ABBEY, MISSION, BC 2016
CROSS DESIGNED BY P. DUNSTAN MASSEY.

49 ST. BENEDICT

THE FATHER OF BENEDICTINE MONKS AND
THE RULE OF ST. BENEDICT.

ST. BENEDICT, PRAY FOR US!

The St. Benedict_Medal is a sacred symbol in the Catholic faith. It is believed to ward against various spiritual and physical afflictions. It is inscribed with powerful prayers and symbols, each with its own specific protective function.

1. To destroy witchcraft and all other diabolical and haunting influences;
2. To impart protection to persons tempted, deluded, or tormented by evil spirits;
3. To obtain the conversion of sinners into the Catholic Church, especially when they are in danger of death;
4. To serve as an armor against temptation;
5. To destroy the effects of poison;
6. To secure a timely and healthy birth for children;
7. To afford protection against storms and lightning;
8. To serve as an efficacious remedy for bodily afflictions and a means of protection against contagious diseases.

Ejus in obitu nostro praesenta mumamar - We desire you in our hour of death to be our armor by your property and presence.

C.S.P.B. - Crux Sancti Patris Benedict - The Cross of Holy Father Benedict

C.S.S.M.L. (usually on the vertical part of the cross-Crux Sancta Sit Mili Lux - May the Holy Cross be my light.

N.D.S.M.D. (usually on the horizontal part of the cross: -Non Drace Sit Mihi Dux - May the dragon be not my leader.

V.R.S. - Vade Retor Satana! - Be gone satan!

N.S.M.V. - Non Suade Mlhl Vana - Entice me not with deceits.

S.M.Q.L. - Sunt mala Quae Libas - What you offered is evil.

I.V.B. - Ipse Venena Bibas = Drink your poison yourself.

Novena to St. Benedict

Glorious St. Benedict who taught us the way to religious perfection by the practice of self-conquest, mortification, humility, obedience, prayer, silence, retirement, and detachment from the world, I kneel at your feet and humbly beg you to take my present need under your special protection (mention here). Vouchsafe to recommend it to the Blessed Virgin Mary, and lay it before the throne of Jesus.

Cease not to intercede for me until my request is granted.

Above all, obtain for me the grace to one day meet God face to face, and with you and Mary and all the angels and saints to praise Him through all eternity.

O most powerful Saint Benedict, do not let me lose my soul, but obtain for me the grace of winning my way to heaven, there to worship and enjoy the most holy and adorable Trinity forever and ever. Amen.

Pray 1 Our Father, 1 Hail Mary, and 1 Glory Be.

Amen.

Prayer to St. Benedict for Protection

O glorious St. Benedict, sublime model of
all virtues,
pure vessel of God's grace! Behold me,
humbly kneeling at thy feet.
I implore thy loving heart to pray for me
before the throne of God.
To thee I have recourse in all the dangers
which daily surround me.
Shield me against my enemies, inspire me
to imitate thee in all things.
May thy blessing be with me always,
so that I may shun whatever God forbids
and avoid the occasions of sin.
Graciously obtain for me from God those
favors and graces of which I stand
so much in need, in the trials, miseries
and afflictions of life.
Thy heart was always so full of love,
compassion, and mercy towards those who
were afflicted or troubled in any way.
Thou didst never dismiss without
consolation and assistance anyone who had
recourse to thee.
I therefore invoke thy powerful
intercession, in the confident hope that thou

wilt hear my prayers and obtain for me the special grace and favor I so earnestly implore (mention it), if it be for the greater glory of God and the welfare of my soul. Help me, O great St. Benedict, to live and die as a faithful child of God, to be ever submissive to His holy will, and to attain the eternal happiness of heaven.

Amen.

O, Holy Father, Saint Benedict, blessed by God in grace and in name, who, while standing in prayer with hands raised to heaven, did most happily yield your angelic spirit into the hands of your Creator, and have promised zealously to defend against all snares of the enemy in the last struggle of death, those who shall daily remind you of your glorious departure in heavenly joys; protect me, I beseech you, O glorious Father, this day and every day by your holy blessings, that I may never be separated from our dear Lord, from your company, and that all the blessed through Christ our Lord, Amen.

The Litany of St. Benedict

Lord, have mercy on us, Christ, have mercy on us.
God the Father of Heaven, Have mercy on us.
God the Son, Redeemer of the world, Have mercy on us.
God, the Holy Spirit, Have mercy on us.
Holy Trinity, One God, Have mercy on us.
litany of st benedict
St. Benedict
Jubilee Medal
Saint Benedict stands on a pedestal, a shepherd's crook in his arm, holding the cross of Jesus in his right hand and his famous Rule in his left. On his right side we see the poisoned cup that could not kill him, and on his left an image of the raven that fed him.
Holy Mary, Pray for us.
Holy Mary, Mother of God, Pray for us.
Holy Virgin of virgins, Pray for us.
Holy Father, Saint Benedict, Pray for us.
Father most reverend, Pray for us.
Father most renowned, Pray for us.
Father most compassionate, Pray for us.

Man of great fortitude, Pray for us.
Man of venerable life, Pray for us.
Man of the most holy conversation, Pray for us.
True servant of God, Pray for us.
Light of devotion, Pray for us.
Light of prayer, Pray for us.
Light of contemplation, Pray for us.
Star of the world, Pray for us.
Best master of an austere life, Pray for us.
Leader of the holy warfare, Pray for us.
Leader and chief of monks, Pray for us.
Master of those who die to the world, Pray for us.
Protector of those who cry to thee, Pray for us.
Wonderful worker of miracles, Pray for us.
Revealer of the secrets of the human heart, Pray for us.
Master of spiritual discipline, Pray for us.
Companion of the patriarchs, Pray for us.
Equal of the prophets, Pray for us.
Follower of the Apostles, Pray for us.
Teacher of Martyrs, Pray for us.
Father of many pontiffs, Pray for us.
Gem of abbots, Pray for us.
Glory of Confessors, Pray for us.

Imitator of anchorites, Pray for us.
Associate of virgins, Pray for us.
Colleague of all the Saints, Pray for us.
Lamb of God, Who takest away the sins
of the world, Spare us, O Lord.
Lamb of God, Who takest away the sins of
the world, Graciously hear us, O Lord.
Lamb of God, Who takes away the sins of
the world, Have mercy on us.
V. Intercede for us, O holy father Saint
Benedict,
R. That we may be made worthy of the
promises of Christ.
Let Us Pray: O God, Who hast called us
from the vanity of the world, and Who dost
incite us to the reward of a heavenly
vocation under the guidance of our holy
patriarch and founder, Saint Benedict,
inspire and purify our hearts and pour forth
on us Thy grace, whereby we may persevere
in Thee. Through Jesus Christ, Our Lord.
Amen.

<u>Prayer to St. Benedict</u>

O Holy Father, St. Benedict, blessed.
By God in grace and in name,
who, while standing in prayer, with
hands raised to heaven, did most happily
yield your angelic spirit into the hands of
your Creator, and have promised zealously
to defend against all the snares of the
enemy in the last struggle of death,
those who shall daily remind you of your
glorious departure and heavenly joys;
protect me, I beseech you,
O glorious Father,
this day and every day, by your holy
blessings, that I may never be separated
from our dear Lord,
from your company, and that of all the
blessed.
Through Christ our Lord.
Amen.

Westminster Abbey, Mission, BC, 2012.

The stained-glass windows within the Monastery.

Inside the church

Westminster Abbey Grounds. Mission, BC, 2013.

50 SUFFERING

"For to you, it has been granted for Christ's sake, not only to believe in Him, but also to suffer for His sake." (Philippians 1:29).

Suffering, there are times we cry out why God? We did not understand the reasoning and questioning period and wondered if we did wrong.

Wondering why we must suffer. Why doesn't the pain get better?

There are so many whys. Why are there so many whys?

There are times we experience these moments when we are knocked down to our knees and cannot get back up.

We pray, and we pray, and it does not go away. The pain day in and day out.

Suffering and sometimes no longer remembering what it feels like not to be in pain to not suffer.

Yet with suffering, there are many who come before us, Saint Faustina, St. Maximilian Kobe, St. Gemma Galgani, and many other saints and people within the world.

We suffer, but it is never in vain—the cries of anguish, tears-stained cheeks, pleading, and begging.

Unite your suffering to Christ. People often wonder about suffering, why people suffer, and why some suffer, and others do not.

Perspective is a part of the equation for those who wonder. Suffering is not always visible; it can be invisible. Pain can be masked and hidden beneath a smile.

We cannot always tell what challenges or suffering someone is facing just by looking at them. I suppose that is where the saying "Don't judge a book by its cover" applies to people.

Invisible, you do not look sick. You cannot really be in pain.

Suffering and redemptive suffering unite us in our sufferings up to Christ and his suffering upon the cross.

It has a reason and a purpose; one we may not understand until the day we stand face-to-face with Christ in heaven. Then, all will be revealed. It will all be made clear.

51 ST. FAUSTINA

Saint Faustina handwrote six notebooks during the time God spoke to her, giving her visions and the message of Divine Mercy. Numerous prayers are in these notebooks, which were turned into a 700-page printed book, *Diary: Mercy in My Soul.*

Pope John Paul II canonized St. Maria Faustina Kowalska as a saint on April 30, 2000. He declared the second Sunday of Easter as Divine Mercy Sunday.

Pope John Paul II Said, *"I wish solemnly to entrust the world to divine mercy. I do so with the burning desire that the message of God's merciful love, proclaimed here through St. Faustina, may be made known to all the peoples of the earth and fill their hearts with hope."*

St. Pope John Paul II was highly devoted to Divine Mercy and spreading the messages Christ gave to St. Faustina.

Christ visited Saint Faustina. She was a young Polish nun who experienced these visions of Christ, and he asked her to tell the world his infinite love and mercy.

Saint Faustina was asked to keep a record of these visions in our diary, which we now have as the diary of St. Faustina.

In one such vision, Jesus asked her to make a painting that portrayed him.

"Paint an image according to the pattern you see, with the signature: 'Jesus, I trust in you.' I desire that this image be venerated, first in your chapel, and then throughout the world. I promise that the soul that will venerate this image will not perish."

ST. FAUSTINA' CONVENT, KRAKOW POLAND 2016.

My mother's side of the family is Polish. So, I have always had an appreciation for Polish saints and history.

When I was a child, my mom went to Poland. She found a great love for St. Faustina and shared it with us upon her return.

I have always loved how St. Faustina was able to experience such amazing God Instances.

I love how God used those instances and worked through her to share his message.

I had the opportunity to visit St. Faustina convent and the Divine Mercy sanctuary during World Youth Day.

[Jesus said,] I am offering people a vessel with which they are to keep coming for graces to the fountain of mercy. That vessel is this image with the signature: "Jesus, I trust in You." (Diary.327).

*DIVINE MERCY SANCTUARY, KRAKÓW,
POLAND 2016.*

ST. FAUSTINA, PRAY FOR US!

OUTSIDE DIVINE MERCY SANCTUARY,
KRAKÓW, POLAND 2016.

DIVINE MERCY CONVENT, KRAKÓW,
POLAND 2016.

INSIDE DIVINE MERCY SANCTUARY,
KRAKÓW, POLAND 2016.

OUTSIDE OF ST. FAUSTINA'S CONVENT.
WITH ONE OF THE SISTERS. POLAND, 2016.

52 DIVINE MERCY

"Look into My Heart and see there the love and mercy which I have for humankind, and especially for sinners. Look and enter into My Passion." Jesus to Saint Faustina. (Diary.1663).

The Divine Mercy is for all who seek it. There can be hardships in life. We are not perfect. Christ's mercy is ever so divine. His love for us is overflowing. Mercy is available to all.

All who approach Christ and ask his mercy to bid him to grant leniency. Divine Mercy, we all need it. We are human; we have faults and weaknesses, and we fall to sin and temptations.

Christ offers us forgiveness, redemption, and mercy. You will never turn us away. We do not have to remain there even if we have fallen into darkness.

Seek mercy and seek Christ and his light within the darkness. Let us be merciful and live our lives with forgiveness within our hearts.

Prayer for Consecration to the Divine Mercy

Jesus, the Divine Mercy, I consecrate my entire life, from this day on to You without reserve. Into Your hands, I abandon my past, present, and future. From this day forward, make me a true follower of Your teaching. Let Your Divine Mercy Image protect my home and my family from all the powers of evil in this world today. May all who venerate it never perish; may it be their joy in life, their hope in death, and their glory in eternity. Amen.

God, merciful Father, in your Son, Jesus Christ, You have revealed your love and poured it out upon us in the Holy Spirit, the Comforter. We entrust to You today the destiny of the world and of every man and woman. Bend down to us sinners, heal our weakness, conquer all evil, and grant that all the peoples of the earth may experience Your mercy. In You, the Triune God, may they ever find the source of hope. Eternal Father, by the Passion and Resurrection of Your Son, have mercy on us and upon the whole world! Amen.

53 THE CHAPLET OF DIVINE MERCY

Jesus told St. Faustina, "I am giving you three ways of exercising mercy towards your neighbor: The first by deed. The second is by word, and the third is by prayer. In these three degrees is contained the fullness of mercy, and it is an unquestionable proof of love for me." (Diary.742).

The Chaplet of Divine Mercy has always been one of my favorite prayer chaplets.

It is a beautiful devotion and a prayer for those in distress and struggling with sins and temptations.

In her diary, St. Faustina shared much about Christ's love and mercy. She explained how praying to the Divine Mercy and praying the chaplet can save souls and open the doors of mercy.

Pray the Divine Mercy. It is necessary to save one's soul and help the Holy Souls in purgatory.

Chaplet of Divine Mercy

JESUS PROMISES GREAT GRACES THROUGH THESE PRAYERS:

O Blood and Water, which gushed forth from the Heart of Jesus as a fount of mercy for us, I trust in You! (3x)

Chaplet of Divine Mercy

On rosary beads, begin: *Our Father, Hail Mary, the Creed.*

On the Our Father beads, *pray: Eternal Father, I offer You the Body and Blood, Soul and Divinity of Your dearly beloved Son, Our Lord Jesus Christ, in atonement for our sins and those of the whole world.*

On the Hail Mary beads, *pray: For the sake of His sorrowful Passion, have mercy on us and on the whole world.*

In conclusion, *pray three times: Holy God, Holy Mighty One, Holy Immortal One, have mercy on us and on the whole world.*

(Offer these prayers at 3:00 p.m., if possible.)

54 LITANY OF DIVINE MERCY

Divine Mercy, gushing forth from the bosom of the Father, Jesus, I trust in You.
*Divine Mercy, greatest attribute of God, **Jesus I trust in You.***
*Divine Mercy, incomprehensible mystery, **Jesus, I trust in You**.*
*Divine Mercy, fountain gushing forth from the mystery of the Most Blessed Trinity, **Jesus, I trust in You.***
*Divine Mercy, unfathomed by any intellect, human or angelic, **Jesus, I trust in You.***
*Divine Mercy, from which wells forth all life and happiness, **Jesus, I trust in You.***
*Divine Mercy, better than the heavens, **Jesus, I trust in You.***
*Divine Mercy, source of miracles and wonders, **Jesus I trust in You.***
*Divine Mercy, encompassing the whole universe, **Jesus, I trust in You.***
*Divine Mercy, descending to earth in the Person of the Incarnate Word, **Jesus, I trust in You.***
Divine Mercy, which flowed out from the

*open wound of the Heart of Jesus, **Jesus, I trust in You.***
*Divine Mercy, enclosed in the Heart of Jesus for us, and especially for sinners, **Jesus, I trust in You.***
*Divine Mercy, unfathomed in the institution of the Sacred Host, **Jesus, I trust in You.***
*Divine Mercy, in the founding of the Holy Church, **Jesus, I trust in You.***
*Divine Mercy, in the Sacrament of Holy Baptism, **Jesus, I trust in You.***
*Divine Mercy, in our justification through Jesus Christ, **Jesus, I trust in You.***
*Divine Mercy, accompanying us through our whole life, **Jesus I trust in You.***
*Divine Mercy, embracing us, especially at the hour of death, Jesus, **I trust in You.***
*Divine Mercy, endowing us with immortal life, **Jesus, I trust in You.***
*Divine Mercy, accompanying us every moment of our life, **Jesus I trust in You.***
*Divine Mercy, shielding us from the fire of hell, **Jesus, I trust in You.***
*Divine Mercy, in the conversion of hardened sinners, **Jesus I trust in You.***
Divine Mercy, astonishment for Angels,

incomprehensible to Saints, **Jesus, I trust in You.**
Divine Mercy, unfathomed in all the mysteries of God, **Jesus, I trust in You.**
Divine Mercy, lifting us out of every misery, **Jesus I trust in You.**
Divine Mercy, source of our happiness and joy, **Jesus I trust in You.**
Divine Mercy, in calling us forth from nothingness to existence, **Jesus, I trust in You.**
Divine Mercy, embracing all the works of His hands, **Jesus, I trust in You.**
Divine Mercy, crown of all God's handiwork, **Jesus I trust in You.**
Divine Mercy, in which we are all immersed, **Jesus, I trust in You.**
Divine Mercy, sweet relief for anguished hearts, **Jesus I trust in You.**
Divine Mercy, only hope of despairing souls, **Jesus I trust in You.**
Divine Mercy, repose of hearts, peace amidst fear, **Jesus, I trust in You.**
Divine Mercy, delight, and ecstasy of holy souls, Jesus, **I trust in You.**
Divine Mercy, inspiring hope against all hope, **Jesus, I trust in You.**

Let us pray:

Eternal God, in whom mercy is endless and the treasury of compassion inexhaustible, look kindly upon us and increase Your mercy in us, that in difficult moments we might not despair nor become despondent, but with great confidence submit ourselves to Your holy will, which is Love and Mercy itself. Amen.

<u>Prayer to be merciful.</u>

Help me, O Lord, that my eyes may be merciful, so that I may never suspect or judge from appearances, but look for what is beautiful in my neighbor's souls. And come to their rescue.

Help me, O Lord, that my ears may be merciful so that I may give heed to my neighbor's needs and not be indifferent to their pains and moaning's.

Help me, O Lord, that my tongue may be merciful, so that I should never speak negatively of my neighbor, but have a word of comfort and forgiveness for all.

Help me, O Lord, that my hands be merciful and filled with the good deeds, so that I may do only good to my neighbors

and take upon myself the more difficult and toilsome tasks.
Help me, O Lord, so that my feet may be merciful so that I may hurry to assist my neighbor, overcoming my own fatigue and weariness.
Help me, O Lord, that my heart may be merciful so that I may feel all the sufferings of my neighbor. May your mercy, Lord, rest upon me.
Amen.

Prayer of Entrustment to Divine Mercy

O Lord, our God.
We place our trust in You,
Because you are mercy itself.
We repent of our sins and turn to You for mercy.
We trust You to provide for our every need according to Your will.
Help us to forgive others as You forgive us.
We promise to be merciful by our deeds, words, and prayers.
Though we have fears because of human weakness, we rely on Your infinite goodness

and mercy.
We entrust to You the future of our
planet, our Church, our nations, our
families, and all our needs.
With loud cries, we implore your mercy
on us and on the whole world.
Look upon us, created in your image and
likeness.
Form us in the Heart of Mary by the
power of the Holy Spirit into the living
images of mercy.
May all come to know the depth of Your
mercy and sing the praises of Your mercy
forever.
Amen!

DIVINE MERCY, PRAY FOR US!

"[Jesus said,] Souls that make an appeal to My mercy delight Me. To such souls I grant even more graces than they ask. I cannot punish even the greatest sinner if he makes an appeal to My compassion." (Diary.1146).

55 THE DESERT

"I cared for you in the wilderness, in the land of burning heat." (Hosea 13:5).

Sometimes, we wander in the desert spiritually. Sometimes, it is darkness and everything around us, and the devil tries to pull us away from God. During his time in the desert, Jesus was brought to temptations.

We will face temptations and spiritual dryness, doubts, and things that bring us to our knees, things that we least expect. Sometimes, we face pain and sorrows.

We will have moments that cause us to doubt or question.

Despair and loneliness creep in during these times.

When we feel as though we have been abandoned in the darkness, we get lost deeper in our struggles.

These times in the desert are not easy, and they make one wonder if there is something wrong with us or if, perhaps, we did something wrong.

The desert is dry, and no matter how much we thirst, our thirst cannot be quenched. We thirst for Jesus, for he is the true living water. Our souls cry out for Christ. Even when we do not see Him, he is with us within the desert; He will help us find refuge.

THE FIRST COMMUNION CROSS WAS SET UP FOR LENT AND REPRESENTS THE CRUCIFIXION AND THE TIME SPENT IN THE DESERT.

56 CROSSES WE BEAR

The burdens and crosses we bear come in all sorts of sizes.

We never know exactly what crosses we will be called to bear or the crosses those around us carry.

We all know the popular saying about not judging a book by its cover, which is the same for people.

We cannot always see the suffering or inner turmoil within another simply by looking at another.

Sometimes, we will wonder why God has given us a particular cross to bear.

These crosses can be very heavy, yet remember that they all have a purpose, and we must bear them like Christ openly and willingly bore his.

Take that which weighs upon you to the foot of the cross.

Offer up the hardships, the aches and pains, disappointments, and the triumphs and successes to Christ.

Remember that God has a plan, and the crosses we bear in our lives often play a bigger role than we are even aware of.

On Palm Sunday, I like to turn my palms into little crosses of all shapes and sizes.

I think of the burdens I might bear that year and how, even though they might be heavy, looking back, one can see how we learn and grow from them.

How we view the things in our lives and our perspective can make a significant difference.

While we may not always understand the crosses we bear or the why of it all, we are never alone, for Christ Walks beside us, and he will help us lift the crosses and lead us closer to him.

PALM SUNDAY CROSSES.

57 DIFFICULT TIMES

There are times when we are challenged when it all seems impossible. When difficult times appear, we feel like nothing can be fixed. Yet the Lord is in control, and we may not have all the answers right now. But one day, it will all make sense.

We all need that extra push forehand to get back out when we fall down. Life may have many ups and downs, but none will ever be too much for us, for God never gives us something we can't handle or take.

We will always get back up and try again, no matter how often we fall and fail. He will always be there, and he will always be with us. He loves us so very much.

Remember that if you look back from where you are now, you can see all you have overcome.

You can see where God worked in your life and where He asked you to wait—the moments when tough times taught us things that helped us with something even harder down the road.

God moments can be widespread in our

lives; sometimes, they are easier to see than others. Life has a way of getting away from us, and there are things in the world that can pull us away from Christ.

Learning to make time for God and put Him at the center of our lives can be challenging when so many things are trying to pull us away from Him.

God will challenge us, and sometimes, we will face challenging times, trials, and difficulties.

Yet if we keep our eyes, hearts, and minds on Christ, those things will not be as difficult as they could be. The Lord does not ever give us something we cannot bear the burden of. Life can be full of things we do not understand, and it can be difficult to find balance in all of it.

So, remember, even during tough times, there is a time and a place, and life does not run on our own timing. It runs on the Lords.

Sometimes, we face these difficult times for a purpose we do not understand. The Lord understands, so put your trust in him during the tough times, and all will be well.

58 HOPE'S STRENGTH

"For My yoke is easy, and My burden is light." (Matthew 11:30).

Like a butterfly emerging from the ashes and rubble, hope has the transformative power to bring light amidst despair.

In moments of tragedy, we witness the resilience of the human spirit. Some succumb to their fears, but others rise with unwavering determination, a beacon of hope in the darkest of times.

There is a unique strength that blossoms within those who are brave. Each of us must discover and nurture our own inner strength, a source of empowerment and confidence.

Hope can be the light that guides us in the darkness. Just a spark of hope can aid one in overcoming even the darkest of times.

Think of the caterpillar; it goes into its cocoon and then needs to use all of its strength to emerge from the cocoon as a butterfly. If someone helps the struggling caterpillar as it tries to emerge from the cocoon, the butterfly will not be able to fly.

The same applies to us. Sometimes, God gives us our own burdens, our cocoon that we must get through first to be able to fly or do what we have been created to do.

Think of ashes of burnt palms on Ash Wednesday, how we are marked with ashes on our forehead as a sign of penance for our sins. A continuous cycle of Christ's light of hope path and its strength.

We emerge from the ashes and become renewed just as we emerge from a cocoon and take flight.

Hope's strength is the strength to continue forward despite the circumstances. Hope exists even in the darkness.

Seek the light and let it guide you. May your burden be light as you walk hand in hand with Christ.

"We wait in hope for the Lord; he is our help and our shield. In him our hearts rejoice, for we trust in his holy name. May your unfailing love be with us, Lord, even as we put our hope in you." (Psalm 33:20-22).

59 IN THE GARDEN

"For as the earth bringeth forth her bud, and as the garden causeth the things that are sown in it to spring forth; so, the Lord God will cause righteousness and praise to spring forth before all the nations." (Isaiah 61:11).

When I turned eleven, I discovered many unexpected God Instances in France. During that pilgrimage, my faith journey grew enormously. It was a significant starting point when I actively started noticing God Instances and moments in my life.

Gardens can have many ties to faith and God, allowing us to draw closer to God within nature and his creations.

The Bible has many stories and parables about gardens and sowing seeds.

For example, the garden of Gethsemane played a significant role in Christ's journey.

We saw the Garden of Eden with Adam and Eve. When we think of gardens, we think of soil, sowing seeds of faith, and planting fruits and vegetables to nourish our hearts and bodies.

The parable of the trusting farmer tills the soil and plants the seeds.

I had my own encounter in the Garden of Nevers, a garden housed within the cloistered convent St. Bernadette entered after her encounters with Our Lady of the Immaculate Conception. This garden, with its serene beauty and rich history, became a place where I found much to bring me closer to God.

I found much to bring me closer to God within this garden. I found a heart stone at the feet of Our Lady.

NEVERS FRANCE, CONVENT GARDEN 2008.

St. Bernadette heard the prayers of a lonely little girl and brought her a friend. Within the garden, the two girls played and laughed.

We were walking the grounds following in the footsteps where St. Bernadette once walked.

God Instances, as I've come to understand them, are those moments when we see God's hand at work in our lives, often in unexpected ways. These are the moments that strengthen our faith and remind us of God's presence in our lives.

NEVERS, FRANCE, CONVENT GARDENS, 2008.

NEVERS, FRANCE, CONVENT GARDENS, 2008.

60 THE POWER OF BOOKS

"And that from a child thou hast known the holy scriptures, which can make thee wise unto salvation through faith which is in Christ Jesus." (2 Timothy 3:15).

The written word has power. Some say words can be dangerous and cannot be taken back once spoken.

When it comes to words, I think of my younger self struggling with reading, dyslexia, and writing.

During my time in France, I experienced the transformative power of books. Everywhere I went, I encountered these little books or booklets about the Saints or the places we visited. These books ignited a deep desire to read more than ever before. This newfound love for reading, especially about the lives of the Saints, became a significant part of my spiritual growth, opening my eyes to the richness of our faith and the inspiring lives of the Saints. Books, especially those that share the wisdom and experiences of the Saints, can be powerful tools for spiritual growth and understanding.

So rather than collecting all kinds of souvenirs or trinkets, I collected books and saint medals.

It seems fitting that I now draft my own book on saints and God instances.

To finish this book, I want to remind you how special books can be and how vital it is for young people to read the stories of the Saints.

We think about books and their role within the church.

Our greatest book and guide is the Bible.

The Bible is God's word at our fingertips. It is a book filled with wisdom and a place to always turn to in all seasons of life.

It is important to note that not everyone uses the same Bible translation version.

The KJV- (King James Version), NIV – (New International Version), NKJV - (New King James Version), and NRSV - (New Revised Standard Version) Are some of the most used translations of the Bible.

I have always liked seeing the distinctive styles of translations.

I primarily use KJV and NIV translations in this book because I like the language style.

It is worth noting that the original King James Bible version had all the same books as the Catholic version.

Sometimes, different translations change the meanings of words, allowing one to connect to a scripture or passage in a separate way.

As a lover of the thesaurus, I see how the meaning behind a word can completely change the context of a sentence.

61 END NOTE

While I am not an expert on faith or saints, I am still learning and growing in faith, and there is always more to learn.

I am blessed and grateful for the opportunity to share my stories and experiences with you.

I am a practicing Catholic, not perfect, and I am still learning and taking time to understand the depths of my faith.

I long to share all these incredible God Instances with others that the Lord has blessed me with.

I have struggled and doubted God's plan for me over the years. I have been lost and broken.

I have faced suffering, and through it all, I have continued to learn about my faith and about God's love and mercy.

God Instances are all around us. We just might not always recognize them.

Everything we face has a purpose, such as love and loss. Before me, Rudy's death, along with Betty's and others I have lost over the years, have taught me about life and death and how God can use it to impact others' lives.

The Saints, with their diverse life experiences and unwavering faith, have been a source of inspiration and guidance for me.

They are examples of many different walks of life, circumstances, and struggles.

We can learn from them about how they faced those various challenges.

We can learn from them about how they faced those different challenges.

As we learn about those Saints and get to know them, we can find how our lives are intertwined, how we face some of the same things, and that we, too, can strive for the path of sainthood.

How we react to our circumstances and actions in situations plays a role in our life journey.

Living a Catholic life takes practice.

We are practicing Catholic because we are practicing.

We are still learning.

We are not perfect, but we will continue to learn, for there is always more to learn about our faith, ourselves, and our relationship with God.

While society will try to pull us away from God, we are living a life of faith or a path that leads us to heaven.

We must hold fast and stand firm in our faith.

There is much to learn in our faith, and we never know how long we will have on this earth.

Our brief time on this earth prepares us for eternal life with God.

Remember, God can work within us in all ways and circumstances, including the most unexpected of ways.

His presence is constant, and His love for us is unwavering.

Be open to His guidance and trust in His plan for you.

I strongly encourage you to delve into books on saints, read the Bible, and explore your faith.

This journey of self-discovery and spiritual growth is a rewarding one, and I am here to support you every step of the way.

Most of all, be open to Christ.

Allow him to enter your life, take time to

be grateful, and trace and recollect your own God moments and Instances.

"It is Jesus, in fact, that you seek when you dream of happiness. He is waiting for you when nothing else you find satisfies you."
St. Pope John Paul II.

May God Bless you and all who read this book.

SMILE GOD LOVES YOU!

God Instances

ABOUT THE AUTHOR

Ruby Nazaruk is the creative mind behind captivating literary works such as "Words in All Their Splendor," "A String Called Love," "A Journey of People & Ourselves," and "Do You Have a Pen? A Trail of What if's & Love." She is also the author of The Author's Mind, Bedtime Stories for Children, and *Leaves & Their Whispers.*

Born and raised in the beautiful landscapes of rural Alberta, Ruby currently calls Edmonton, Alberta, home. Armed with a B.A. in history and a minor in political science, she brings a unique perspective to her writing.

For Ruby, writing is more than a skill—it is a passion cultivated over the years, alongside her love for reading and avid bookworm. Beyond her literary pursuits, Ruby profoundly affectionates her Catholic faith, seizing every opportunity to share her experiences and beliefs. In her words and tales, Ruby strives to leave an indelible mark on hearts and minds alike.

www.ingramcontent.com/pod-product-compliance
Lightning Source LLC
Chambersburg PA
CBHW022127050726
47590CB00002B/437